The Life
You Deserve

Step by Step Guide to
Passion, Purpose & Profits

First published by O Books, 2009
O Books is an imprint of John Hunt Publishing Ltd., The Bothy, Deershot Lodge, Park Lane, Ropley,
Hants, SO24 0BE, UK
office1@o-books.net
www.o-books.net

Distribution in:	South Africa
	Alternative Books
UK and Europe	altbook@peterhyde.co.za
Orca Book Services	Tel: 021 555 4027 Fax: 021 447 1430
orders@orcabookservices.co.uk	
Tel: 01202 665432 Fax: 01202 666219	Text copyright Shelley Kaehr 2008
Int. code (44)	
	Design: Stuart Davies
USA and Canada	
NBN	ISBN: 978 1 84694 207 5
custserv@nbnbooks.com	
Tel: 1 800 462 6420 Fax: 1 800 338 4550	All rights reserved. Except for brief quotations
	in critical articles or reviews, no part of this
Australia and New Zealand	book may be reproduced in any manner without
Brumby Books	prior written permission from the publishers.
sales@brumbybooks.com.au	
Tel: 61 3 9761 5535 Fax: 61 3 9761 7095	The rights of Shelley Kaehr as author have been
	asserted in accordance with the Copyright,
Far East (offices in Singapore, Thailand,	Designs and Patents Act 1988.
Hong Kong, Taiwan)	
Pansing Distribution Pte Ltd	
kemal@pansing.com	A CIP catalogue record for this book is available
Tel: 65 6319 9939 Fax: 65 6462 5761	from the British Library.

Printed by Digital Book Print

O Books operates a distinctive and ethical publishing philosophy in
all areas of its business, from its global network of authors to
production and worldwide distribution.

The Life You Deserve

Step by Step Guide to
Passion, Purpose & Profits

Shelley Kaehr, Ph.D.

BOOKS

Winchester, UK
Washington, USA

CONTENTS

Acknowledgements

This book is dedicated to the hundreds of students I've worked with through the years who shared their time and energy with me.

I also wish to acknowledge the following people:

Linnea Armstrong, Cindy Kennedy, Brenda Bischoff, Pat Moon, Paula Wagner, Tammy Ledbetter, the late Father Paul Keenan, Jim Merideth, Keith Sniadach, Will Rosasco.

Thanks to John Hunt of O Books for his belief in this project, Trevor Greenfield for editing support and Maria Watson.

Above all, thanks to my parents, Mickey and Gail, and my brother, Mark.

There are no words to express my gratitude to each of you.

Thank You!

Part One
Our Role in the World

Introduction

For the past several years I have been working in the field of alternative therapies helping people let go of their past and find the potential for a bright, powerful future within them. My message has always been the same: you are creating your life, your reality, with your thoughts.

I have always believed that we all have a powerfully innate wisdom within us that knows at the deepest levels what is best for us, what will make us happy and what will allow our souls to feel as though we are contributing something special to the world around us.

During a recent trip to India, however, my core beliefs were turned upside down after a powerful encounter with some special astrologers who seemed to know every single thing about me, down to the smallest details.

I was presenting my research into parallel universes to an international gathering of hypnotherapists in New Delhi when I met a friend who told me she was going to have a special reading done called a Naadi Leaf reading.

She planned to travel to the south to have it done after the conference was over.

"What is a Naadi Leaf reading?" I asked.

'They take your thumbprint and if they find your information they can tell you every single thing about your life. It's like a soul record," she said.

"Deepak Chopra talked about it in one of his books and said they knew everything about him, including the exact time of his father's death," she added.

"Can it be done in Delhi?" I asked.

"I think so," she said, "I'll have to check."

I was intrigued, to say the least, so I did some research on my own. Naadi astrology was developed over two thousand years ago and began as the simple task of writing information down about everyone who was alive at the time, recording the information on palm leaves.

The records talk about the person's lifetimes in the past and future and everything in between. Only a handful of people have this information on record since this was something that was initially done only for those people living in India at the time.

The records were disbursed and eventually found their way to a family in southern India who made it their sacred duty to preserve, protect and carry on the information for subsequent generations.

The text was written in Tamil, a dead language, and like a shaman passing the sacred information on to his predecessor, the gift of reading the leaves was passed down from generation to generation.

A couple days into the conference my friend rushed up to me, breathless.

"Where have you been?" she said. "I've been looking all over for you. I found a Naadi Leaf reader and I think they just found my leaves. They're still looking for them!"

My inner voice told me to leave immediately and I took a cab to the place where she had the reading done. The cab wound through the huge city and into a residential area where the Naadi Leaf readers lived in an upstairs apartment.

I remember when I arrived there was a most compassionate man standing on the porch, looking right at me. The excitement in my gut told me I was in the right place, but for what, I had no idea.

When I went into the lobby, the only requirement was that I put my thumbprint on a pad of paper. They did not want my name or any other information about me. Then they took the thumbprint upstairs and began to search.

I have always thought it is miraculous that there is nobody else on earth who has the same fingerprints as you do. We are truly a unique expression of creation, and the leaf readers honored that. If my leaves were indeed, in this place, there would be nobody else just like me.

After about twenty minutes they came back to tell me they thought they found my leaves. I was pleased, although I really didn't know what it all meant.

Two men led me into a room with a couple of chairs and a small table and told me to wait. I felt like I was at a doctor's office waiting for the exam.

Soon, the door opened and the kind man who met me when I first arrived walked in with a younger man who obviously did not speak any English.

The older man explained that he was the translator because the younger man had been given the gift of being able to translate the meanings of the leaves, passed down through eight generations of his family.

The Naadi Leaves are written on palm leaves bound at both ends with a piece of twine. They are shaped like an incense box – about ten inches long by a couple inches wide with rounded edges. I could see the writing on them, but it was in an unfamiliar script and it just looked like scribble to me.

The reader sat and closed his eyes and began to pray. Once his prayer was made, he went into an altered state, chanting in sounds I had never heard before. Then he would say something in Hindi and my translator would relay it to me.

"Your name is Joan," the translator said.

"No, that's not me," I said.

He relayed the information to the reader who flipped to the next leaf down and began again.

"Your mother has the name of a Greek goddess," he said.

I thought about this one for a minute and started to say 'no' until I remembered that since she goes by her middle name, her first name is, indeed, that of a Greek goddess.

"Yes," I said.

The process of elimination went rather slowly; with each confirmation, I was told never to give more than a yes or no answer. Finally an entire stack of leaves had been read and although these people, whoever they were, seemed to have a lot in common with me, they were not me. The adventure, I assumed, was over. In a way, I was disappointed, although I didn't really know why, since I had no clue what it was I was expecting to find.

They told me to wait there and both left the room. Within five minutes they were back again with another stack of leaves and asked me to follow them across the hall into another room where the process began again.

With the second stack, the things they asked seemed to get much more specific. They knew about some health problems I had suffered many years ago, they knew my profession, my father's profession and about my brother who is mildly autistic.

Still, I was a bit skeptical until the man who could not speak any English at all spoke my father's name aloud.

"Mi- Kee," he said, doing his best to pronounce a name I am sure he'd never heard before. "Your father's name is Mickey," the translator said.

At that moment, the blood seemed to rush from my body and my jaw hit the table. I felt a cold chill go down my spine. I wondered how they could possibly know that. It was way too uncanny, and at that moment, I felt they really did have some information about me.

Once I nodded in speechless consent to the name of my father, on that same leaf they told me the exact hour of my birth and the date and even day of week. They had never met me before, and had no access to any kind of electronic astrological data, and they could not have known it anyway because I never revealed it.

I was staring my own destiny in the face and it was a much more frightening thing than I would have ever imagined.

I think it is common for us to want to know about our future, sometimes. Our curiosity about what will happen if we do this or that is the kind of information that has kept amateur psychics in business throughout the ages. In this case, it seemed these people really had my number. Not just some random nonsense about whether this relationship would work or if that business deal would go through. They knew about *me*, and it scared me to death — speaking of which, these astrologers can often tell a person exactly when their number is going to be up, which is something I was not sure I really wanted to know, especially if it was sooner, rather than later.

Once the exact leaf is found, it is only part of a larger record so I made an appointment to come back a couple days later to hear the rest of the information. I hated having to wait two whole days, but my presentation to the convention was on the following day and I did not want this process to interfere.

When I returned to the conference and met up with my friend and told her, she was amazed. The men were still searching for her leaves and as it turned out, through word of mouth, there were seven of us total from the conference, including my friend, who all found our leaves at this place over those next few days.

The likelihood of this happening was like finding a needle in a haystack, from the research I did on it. The leaves were all one-of-a-kind and spread all over India, but primarily housed in the south. Just because your leaves showed up in one location did not mean they were in any other. It is not a computerized database at all. This coincidence was truly extraordinary.

I began to think about the implications of such information. Eons ago, sages put pen to paper and recorded incredibly profound information about the destiny of a handful of souls to be picked up at a later time.

It was like leaving a message in a bottle and sending it – not into a space capsule or an underground cavern, but to a specific place in time where it would be discovered only by the specific person who sought it.

The translator told me I was 'destined' to show up to collect my reading before my thirty-ninth birthday, which happened to be that next month.

Philosophically, I had a problem with the word 'destiny' for reasons mentioned at the beginning of this chapter.

I do not believe I am merely the puppet on stage, as Shakespeare suggested, performing on the whims of some puppet master. I believe I am consciously controlling my outcomes with my thoughts and attitudes.

I spoke with my Naadi Leaf readers about this concept at length after they explained this reading would tell me my preordained destiny. "What if I don't believe in destiny?" I asked. "What if I don't want to follow what you tell me?"

"It is your choice," was the answer I received. "It will be more difficult for you than following your path, but it is up to you."

From the sound of these people at our initial meeting, they made each of us feel as though they were going to spell it all out for us – as if the innate wisdom of our very creator would be giving us the exact plan, down to the letter, for our lives.

I think that is why anxiety struck our hearts and the next couple days were extremely challenging and stressful.

At the conference, the word began to spread about all of us who had found our leaves an it created a fascinating philosophical debate on the nature of free will, fate and destiny in our lives.

In the final analysis, I went back two days later, filled with anxiety, to hear what they would tell me. I was happily surprised that the information, although helpful, was not as specific as I had feared it would be.

At that point, it was almost like a road map, marking some of the important stops along the way, while never disclosing the subtle nuances that would color my journey and make it my own.

I was pleased to hear about my long life and the long life of my family and if someone else was told such a thing, I would tell them what I told myself: you are free to accept or reject this information. It holds no power over you.

In the case of my family's well-being and my own long earthly journey, I choose to believe what they told me and I've found that by doing so, it has given me a new sense of peace I did not quite have before. I am here for the long haul.

Did I really need a special astrologer to find inner peace? No, of course not.

The kind of peace I'm talking about in this book is created from within, yet there may be mile markers or things in the outer world that serve either as a reflection to show us how far we've come on our journey or offer gentle reminders, as the Naadi Leaves did for me, of what we know from within us – that we are eternal beings and all is well.

One

Making History

This time in history is particularly interesting to me. We are seeing an incredible shift, particularly over the past decade, in how we view the world around us as things are changing and accelerating at lightning speeds. Sometimes it's hard to keep up.

Our entire social and economic system is slowly turning back to what it once was, only now we have the incredible gifts of technology to assist us like never before.

In the old days, so to speak, everyone worked for themselves. They were entrepreneurs and farmers and they bartered their goods and services and were more self sufficient in many ways.

With the development of automation and the rise of the industrial revolution, individuals were lured away from their own businesses for the hopes and promises that higher pay and supposedly less individual responsibility would bring them. Factories employed most people and the farmer became the exception, not the norm.

As the United States has urbanized over the past century, people who once lived in the city began moving away from urban centers for the hope of a more quiet existence away from their fellow man. For a time, this was a wonderful thing, but now, we have a whole new set of problems developing as a result of our negligence.

Our children, once considered our greatest asset, were being neglected while parents chased the almighty dollar, and now, we can clearly see the damage this neglect is wreaking on our society.

Also, the technology that we have so valued has automated us out of personal relationships altogether. People are isolated, keeping only the company of their computer because it is not necessary anymore to meet with each other face-to-face.

The factories that once supplied the majority with their livelihood are now automating to the point that the people who were once the backbone of their operations are now as obsolete as the farmers once were.

People are panicked to a certain degree because all they have known in their lifetime is working for someone else. Many are faced with the uncertainty of having to quickly find other kinds of work and for many that path is leading them back to where we all came from – entrepreneurship and self-employment.

We also see a new trend in the way we live. Urban populations are beginning to grow again for the first time in decades as more and more people are moving back to the cities.

I spent some years working as membership director for the Lower Downtown Historic District in downtown Denver, Colorado, several years ago.

Denver is considered one of the premier urban development projects in the entire United States. It is a model for cities all over our country.

The insightful citizens of Denver went in years ago to think about how to save the deteriorating city from complete destruction. The old abandoned historical buildings and warehouses were a huge skid row and the homeless population was out of control.

Several conservationists took money from their own pockets to purchase the old buildings and began one of the largest development projects in history, renovating the buildings and turning them into luxury loft condominiums and zoning their area as mixed use, meaning people could come into the area to both live and work so the idea of community and neighborhood could once again prevail.

What happened when our country began to develop the suburbs is that we were so fed up with seeing our neighbors and living near our work and businesses that we began to nationally zone property so that you could either live or work in an area but not both. It sounded like a neat idea at first, but over time, what happened is that our sense of community disappeared and people were forced to get into their cars and drive long distances to get to work or to other necessities.

Once a majority of the population began living like this, traffic problems became, and still are, a huge problem for the majority of our cities; people, in the meantime, were becoming more isolated from each other. After all, who wants to go visit with their neighbors after sitting in traffic for several hours? This concept has taken its toll on the American public.

Several years and millions of dollars later, the Denver project has been an incredibly successful example of how we can reintroduce community into the downtown area and reclaim it once again for future generations.

Now nearly every modern city in America is working on urban development projects similar to the one in Denver and slowly but surely we are recognizing the important fact that we really do need each other.

Things never stay the same and as we are moving back into a lifestyle similar to that of our ancestors, we do so with new eyes and new insights. We are making history!

And when it comes to our topic – finding inner peace – I think we are making great strides as well. Our yearning to rediscover each other is also contributing to the ever-increasing value we place on our spirituality.

As we are faced daily with discouraging headlines, we have turned back to our faith to get us through these trying times with a belief that things will get better.

Concentrated effort at group prayer and meditation seems to be occurring in record numbers and we now have scientific evidence to suggest that our prayers actually have an effect on not only our physical bodies, but on the world around us.

A friend of mine from India was just commenting on this the other day. "There are people in the United States who are really getting to the core of what yoga is really about," he said. "Things are shifting so quickly, pretty soon the American instructors will have to go to India to teach them!"

The fact that we are even at all aware of our connection with the divine is so encouraging to me that we are making tangible progress toward creating the peaceful world we want to live in, and as we continue to evolve our consciousness to accept just how powerful we are in creating all we see around us, we are truly in the midst of not only rewriting history, but literally recreating the way the world operates from the inside out. What an exciting time to be alive!

Two

Hand of Fate

In ancient Greece, the Fates were known as the daughters of Zeus and Themis, mother of necessity. The three women were collectively called the Moirai and named Koltho, Lakhesis and Atropos.

Klotho spins the thread of life while Lakhesis determines its length and Atropos cuts the thread at death.

This ancient rendition of how life works provides powerful imagery as to how our lives unfold day by day, as if some unseen force is guiding us.

What is amazing is how we seem to think that our egos are in total control of things and how we often fail to release and allow a flow of prosperity and abundance to illuminate our lives for the better.

It is not our ego and controlling ways that assist us on our paths, but our willingness to let go and let God, so to speak.

That being said, my entire career has been spent teaching people to believe in themselves and recognize that they have the power to make their lives into whatever kind of creation they want it to be.

The idea that all of the things that happen to us are merely a result of preordination was almost too much for me to believe and yet the Naadi Leaves and their lesson seemed to put that idea in my face in a way that was far more profound than I can ever before recall.

The term fate has always carried a sense of doom with it – the idea that things are fated seems to suggest they cannot be altered and so we mere mortals have little power over what happens to us and that our lot in life is determined solely by the discretion of the Fates.

After the reading I had serious questions on my mind, as did my fellow Naadi Leaf recipients. Are we meant to be born at a particular time and die at a particular time? Are we, indeed, meant to be certain places, meet certain people and do certain things at prearranged places in the time continuum? The Naadi astrologers would like to convince us that is the case.

Recently a friend passed away after being hospitalized for injuries she sustained in a car accident. I remember when I first heard about the accident, I had a bad feeling. Somehow I knew this was a life threatening situation.

A week before her death, I remember I became very ill and the night she died, I got so tired I went to bed right after dinner. The next morning, I got a call from our mutual friend. He did not tell me anything, but something in the sound of his voice told me everything. I saw my friend's face pass in front of my mind's eye, and I knew she was gone.

What is this inner voice that guides us and how is it that we somehow know things before they actually happen? It is as though the voice of the Fates themselves whispers in our ear to tell us things if we are able and willing to listen.

Something about her death more than any other time I can remember made me feel as though there really must be some kind of higher power guiding everything we are doing here and that same power is speaking, or I should say whispering, to us daily, giving us clues and information about what is to come. Not exactly telling us how or why things happen, but telling us subtly about what is to come and when we can accept that, I think a greater sense of peace falls over us.

I used to grieve terribly for my friends who pass away and now I try to sense the divine in it all, that they are truly where they are meant to be and that somehow a higher power had a hand in it all and that all is well.

If we are fated to live a certain amount of time, do specific things and leave earth at a moment in time of our choosing, then what we do in between must be somehow guided by a higher power or force and chosen for us to experience long before we ever arrive here.

Greek and Roman mythology and Naadi Leaf readers would tell us it is not possible to alter the hand of Fate.

Being a proponent of many worlds theory, I still think that we may have the opportunity to choose different fates in different realities. It does seem though, at times, that we have absolutely no control in any of it.

Three

Destiny

Destiny has an air of the magical and impossible. It has a positive connotation about the highest potential for our being and to live up to one's true destiny or calling is a worthy and most high endeavor.

My trip to visit the Naadi Leaf reader left me wondering if I have a preset destiny of things I have come here to accomplish.

I have always believed that each of us is here to do special things. The challenge lies in how we are going to go about accomplishing our destiny. It is often hard to see the forest for the trees and to get on track to where we are supposed to be going.

Because I have been doing intuitive work now for many years, I discovered that I seem to have an ability to look within someone and see their highest potential – who they could be if they were to live up to the grandest manifestation of their lives.

This ability can be seen as both blessing and curse. It is wonderful to look within someone's soul and see the beautiful creation they are, and yet it can be very disappointing to realize that so many people are afraid of stepping out into their destiny and embracing all that life has to offer.

He Wouldn't Live Up to His Potential

The most painful lesson I ever had about this involved someone I dated many years ago. He was an incredibly talented country singer who opened for Garth Brooks and had just as much vocal ability than anyone else on the charts.

It would have been so easy for him to become one of the greatest country singers ever, and yet he was not willing or able

17

to do it. When I first met him I had no idea he was a full blown alcoholic and when asked about it he said he was unwilling to stop. He refused to give up the drinking to have the life he was capable of having.

It makes you wonder how someone could be blessed with such an incredible gift and then choose to throw it and everything else down the drain.

Was it his destiny to become a bum, a chart-topping entertainer, or both? How can we know for sure what was meant to be?

One night I had a dream we were in Nashville and he was accepting an entertainer of the year award. Obviously that never happened in the reality I was living in.

This example and so many others I hear practically daily from my clients, tells me that the many worlds theory makes more sense than ever. It was so easy for me to see this person's potential, and yet it was so easy for him not to live up to that, it makes me wonder if both possibilities existed simultaneously but in separate worlds.

I'm sure if you think about it you can recall someone you know who is clearly not fulfilling their potential. It is heartbreaking to see, but seems to be a part of life.

For most people I think that the feeling of believing you have a higher purpose here on our earth helps you get through the days, stick out the tough times and hang in when the going gets rough. Without the feeling that the things you're going through are helpful and meaningful, I don't think most people could get by.

Four

Who Am I?

I know I must not be the only person on planet earth who has ever woken up in the morning and wondered, 'Who am I?' or 'What is the meaning of my life and all of this that I am doing?' or 'Does my life matter? Am I making a difference?' The list could go on and on, I'm sure.

These perplexing questions are familiar conumdrums for the majority of people who visit me for coaching sessions.

I think it is a deeply ingrained human need to feel wanted, valued and needed and somehow in the midst of all the chaos that constitutes our lives, we all get so bogged down in the inertia of our daily grind that when we have a rare moment to pause, these type of questions seem to pop up and they need to be answered.

In fact, throughout recorded history, man has asked these type questions, and has always come to the same vague conclusions.

I said earlier that I do not think we can ever truly know the mind of God and it is probably not our place to fully understand the world around us and why certain things happen. On a more universal level, to question the meaning of life is something that will engage our hearts and minds through the ages.

These days, more people are questioning not only the universal reason for things, but how they fit into that bigger picture, bringing the question of the meaning or purpose of life to a more personal level.

How can you, as an individual, contribute most productively to the world in the unique way you were intended to? Is there a destiny, as my Naadi Leaf readers suggested, to why each of us is here? What is the unique gift you bring to the world at this time?

I think at a soul level we all used to know who we are, but over time, we've forgotten who that person even is, if we ever were able to adequately express it.

Later in the book in the section on values, you'll see how difficult it is for us to separate our own beliefs from the thoughts and beliefs of those around us. It is often more challenging to hear the inner voice that lovingly guides us to that higher purpose, or reason for being.

This book is designed to assist you in rediscovering yourself and developing a plan of creating more joy in your life and bringing forth the deepest yearnings of your soul.

Inside every person alive is a burning desire or passion for something that you not only love to do, but are very good at. Remembering what that is and finding a way to bring more of that energy into your daily life is the goal of this book.

We all deserve to be happy and have the things we want in life. It's all possible!

For many years, one of the primary reasons people have come to see me is for help discovering what their soul purpose is. Because it is difficult to see ourselves, people often need assistance identifying that special reason they are earth at this time.

Just as our fingerprints are one-of-a-kind reminders of our unique place on the earth, I really believe that each one of us has a special gift within us that is totally unique to who we are and why we are here.

There is something you can do right now better than anyone else on earth. Have you ever stopped to think about that? It's true!

I think these days, more than ever, people are really seeking something, some idea of why they are here and for reasons I talked about earlier, they are seeking this insight in record numbers.

Many have been laid off, or forced to resign from their jobs, and are in the midst of completely redesigning their lives. It is like we, as a population, are coming to, so to speak, from a deep sleep and as we awaken from the fog of what our lives have become, we yearn to find a deeper meaning in our existence, not only for ourselves personally, but for the world at large.

Someone who has worked for the same company for twenty or thirty years who suddenly finds themselves without work is in a serious crisis and often needs direction on where to go with their life.

You may find yourself in a similar situation. I know I did. That is why I got into the work I am in.

For me, it began nearly fifteen years ago when a dear friend of mine was suddenly killed in a hiking accident. I was working at the time for a sales organization and I was miserable, yet like so many of the people I now work with, I was just going through the motions and not doing anything to change my situation. In fact, I can say that I don't even think I was conscious of just how much I was repressing my spirit and ignoring everything that mattered to me. I was waking up every day, doing my job, and going home. Because the money was good, I don't think I paid much attention to anything else. I was in the rut, in the routine of the daily grind.

That came to a screeching halt when I heard about my friend's death. I wondered how this could have happened to someone so young, who had so much to offer the world.

I realized that not only was I not living up to my potential, I was not even enjoying the ride. I wondered if I was in his place and my life was over today how I would feel. Would I be able to say I had seen and done all I had wanted to in this lifetime? My friend talked about going to Europe. He never made it.

It was as if everything I still wanted to do, both personally and professionally, flashed before my eyes, and I knew at that moment that my life was not what I wanted it to be.

Strangely, my deceased friend would often tell me, 'life is

what you make it,' and I could certainly see through his passing that my life, although I was still alive, was certainly not at all what I wanted it to be.

That eye-opener called me to go on years of soul-searching, taking classes, traveling and searching for something to make my life feel like it was more in my control and more the way I would want to make it.

The transformational power of regression therapy, for me, could not be denied, and I was anxious to learn it and help others through this amazing modality.

Now I see the same thing in my clients. They are often struggling, as I once did, with the knowing that they are not doing what makes their soul sing and yet they are in situations where it is difficult to stop on a dime and change directions quickly.

People also struggle with figuring out what it is they would do if they could. I think we all get so desensitized to our own inner voice and soul calling that we cannot even hear it anymore.

Of course, most people will tell you life is tough and you have to sometimes do things that are unpleasant. I have yet to find a career where every single part of the day to day operation of it is a complete 100% joy, but I think the idea here is to find something that is joyful *most* of the time.

That is the goal of this book and of the courses I designed and have taught over the past several years – to help you get into the deepest parts of yourself and figure out what it is that will make your heart sing, give you joy and make you feel that your life is meaningful and worth living.

Later in the book, you will have the opportunity to journey via hypnosis to a space where you can get in touch with the inner part of yourself. It is a powerful process that has helped me, as well as many of my clients, gain clarity and direction in life.

Five

The Power of Choice

At one point during the Naadi Leaf readings, I became almost belligerent as I questioned my messenger and the young man about the information in my reading.

"What if you give me information and I choose not to follow it? Are you saying it will happen anyway, or do I have choice?"

"You can choose to follow this reading, or you can decide not to," he replied. "The path of this destiny we give you is not necessarily easier, but it is the lighter path. If you choose not to follow it, that is your decision, but it will not be as easy."

The answer satisfied me simply because it reminded me of some of the things I have discussed with my clients in the past.

Often people come to me because they have a decision to make and somehow cannot decide which choice is best.

In this case I have them imagine they are traveling out to their possible future, noticing it as a beam of light that they are floating over. At some point in the future line, I have them imagine it branches off into a fork in the road so it is easy for them to notice. Each branch of the fork represents a decision they made and I want them to notice which is lighter or brighter. When they do that, and they always can, they will be able to tell themselves which decision is best for them to follow, and hopefully can make a more educated decision about which to do.

Knowing what I know about how powerful this process can be for helping people make tough decisions, I was surprised by my own reactions to what I was hearing in the reading.

For some reason, this Naadi Leaf reading seemed more real to me than simply traveling in my mind to imaginary futures. Maybe that was because it was here, in the physical plane where someone was holding the message, reading it and telling me so many things I could never have thought anyone would know about me. The reality of the whole thing really brought up some powerful issues, not only for me, but for the others on my journey.

In my earlier work, *Beyond Reality: Evidence of Parallel Universes*, I documented the case histories of my hypnosis clients who were taken into completely new 'realities' via hypnosis so they could heal from profound medical conditions and basically begin anew.

Because I am an enthusiastic student of all of the new thoughts in physics, I believe that there are many realities begin played out simultaneously and it is up to us which one to focus our attention on at any given time.

I've hosted my own radio program for many years by the same name, Beyond Reality, and shortly after my journey in India, I interviewed the renowned physicist, Dr Fred Alan Wolf.

I decided it would be interesting to get his opinion of the events in India since his mind is so scientifically oriented.

His response was no surprise. Dr Wolf believes that the 'coincidence' of the Naadi leaves and the fact that I was 'destined' to be there before age thirty nine was merely one possibility in the realm of all possibilities.

Had I not been there to observe that, another reality would have unfolded and I would not have been any the wiser. I would not have been affected and would never have noticed the new paradigm shifts that occurred, something else would have happened instead, and in some other world, something else *did* happen.

Perhaps I just stayed home and worked with my coaching clients, went to speak at a different conference or any number of other possibilities. That is the beauty of this kind of thinking, and the difficulty in it – there are no definitive answers to exactly what those other possibilities could have been.

When I guide my clients into their possible futures, for

example, they are seeing only one path leading them toward a bright future, and yet there could be unlimited numbers of other possibilities awaiting them depending on their choices.

It's an answer I expected from Dr Wolf, and yet, at the same time, I did not want to hear it. I was still so overcome by the whole thing at the time of our conversation and I think I have always enjoyed the idea of believing that my life is the magical unfolding of my unique destiny and contribution to the world, and I did not want scientific evidence getting in the way of my pie-in-the-sky fantasies.

And yet, I realize my life was not always that way. I've had very hard times, as I know you have, and that is why I believe that no matter how difficult things get for each of us through the years, that there is always hope that life can and will get better.

If you were to tell me about tough times and things you are going through right now, I could help you to see the other possibilities, that life really is a wonderful place to be and that sometimes the tough times give way to our greater appreciation of the good things in life.

How we do that, I think, is by shifting our attention, or going, if you will, into a new reality where things really are different and more empowering.

Is your life composed of a preordained destiny or a series of choices you make that lead you down a particular path?

I believe the answer to that question is completely unknowable while we are in physical form, yet in my opinion it has to be some combination of the two. Perhaps there is a roadmap created long before we arrive to this time and place and within that roadmap lies all of the major stopping points along the way of our lives.

Within that framework however, the decisions we make, the things we do and the people we meet are all up to us to create. It is all driven by our choices.

If you and I decided to take a trip this summer to England, for example, we could plan the dates, we could even select the sites we wanted to tour, and yet each minute of each day would still unfold in ways that we would find surprising.

That is the power of free will and choice coexisting within the orchestration of a higher power or force that guides us all.

As we go through this book, we will be going through some exercises designed to assist you on your journey to the highest and most peaceful destiny so you can focus your attention on that space more often and begin to live the life you deserve and discover the inner peace you seek.

Six

Making the Commitment

One of the things I have encountered in the business I am in, is the constant struggle people have getting through the day and making wise, powerful choices for themselves. We all want to live better lives and although we seem to have innate wisdom within us, we all need a hand once in awhile to see ourselves and to get the proper information to move forward.

That being said, in my field, I have become increasingly disgusted by how much some people rely on intuitive information from outside sources. It's one thing to consult a psychic or counselor from time to time, but what tends to happen in my business is that people become way too dependent on this information, so much so that they have problems moving forward with tasks as simple as tying their shoes or dressing in the morning without the advice of someone else.

It's as if there are many of us who just don't want to take any kind of responsibility for ourselves and if you get a reading and the person tells you something that doesn't happen, you feel its okay to blame them or tell them they are wrong and that somehow that is why things are not working out.

It's a very frustrating part of my work and one reason why I do not enjoy giving straight intuitive readings anymore.

She Wouldn't Even Drive Around the Block!

I had a girl once who got a reading from me and wanted to know if she would be moving soon. Based on what I could see at that moment, I told her, yes, I could see a move happening within the next six to eight weeks.

Two months later I got a phone call one evening. "Hi, Dr Shelley. I had a reading from you a couple months ago and you told me I would be moving. It hasn't happened yet."

When I get a call like this, there seems to be some kind of expectation that I will wave my wand and suddenly the move, which was delayed, will now happen. Sorry folks, it just doesn't work that way!

I returned her call and decided to ask some simple questions. "After our session did you drive around the neighborhood where you want to live to see if there were any signs out for places to rent?"

Her answer should not have been a surprise, and yet it was. "No," she said.

"Did you check the want ads in the paper?" I asked.

"Well, no," she said.

"Did you call any realtors in the area?" I am sure you see where this is going.

"No," she said.

At this point, I had to become about as direct as I ever am.

"Do you think God Almighty is going to send a bolt of lighting through your living room with a room rental agreement attached to it?"

"Well, uh....I don't know," she said.

"God helps those who help themselves. Have you ever heard that one?" I asked her.

"You asked me if you were going to get to move and you can move and the universe can support you in that, but within that framework, you have to take some action in order to make that happen. Do you understand that?"

She did. In fact, I think she was a bit embarrassed by the whole thing.

This is why I feel hypnosis is a much more empowering form of healing than simply giving out advice because in that modality I am merely your facilitator and you are the one with the pictures, thoughts and feelings in your own mind, in your own frame of reference figuring out how your future will unfold and if you are actively involved in that process, you become more empowered, which is why I've included several guided imagery exercises for you later in the book.

Making the Commitment

Before we really get into things, I want to ask you to do something very important for yourself. Make a commitment, a concept that strikes fear in the hearts of many, yet it is one of the most important things you can do for yourself.

I'm about to ask you to make a commitment to doing what you need to do to get where you want to go. I have found that when my students commit to it in writing, they are more likely to take it seriously and have a greater success rate than those who do not make the commitment.

In the self-help industry the standard time accepted for making substantial change is 30 days. It takes 30 days of doing something to make it a new habit.

This process is no different. You're going to be going on a journey, of sorts, and in that journey, you will be asked to stretch and grow and keep an open mind to all that is possible, and to possibly change.

Does that mean we can't make change sooner than 30 days? Of course! I believe all things are possible. One of the reasons I went into the field of hypnotherapy is because I believe that modality assists people in making permanent shifts instantly. That being said, our minds are complicated, so although hypnosis can make the change instantly, only time will tell if it sticks.

You could decide right now to make some huge change in your life like to stop smoking or to get on an exercise plan, and you could go out today and live in this new way and do just great. It's only after some time has passed, though, and you have lost the desired weight, or haven't smoked in awhile, or whatever, that the change is really powerfully noticeable not only by yourself, but also by others.

So when I say change takes time, don't be discouraged. The biggest part of it is deciding today to do the exercises in the book, notice how they are affecting your life, then making the changes or refinements of your thinking that will help you create the ideal situation for yourself.

Here is the agreement below. I would encourage you to sign this, right here, in this book. Feel free to underline, make notes and do whatever you need to do in the book to make it yours – your program, your outcome.

I'd also like to ask that you get a journal you can keep for making notes in during our time together. I could talk all day about the many benefits of keeping a journal to record your important thoughts. It has been an incredibly helpful habit I've been doing now for over twenty years.

The journal can be any bound pad of paper, a spiral notebook or, the kind I like, a cloth bound book with blank pages inside. Regardless, it doesn't matter the kind or the cost, just get yourself something to write in.

If you are one of the technically savvy people in the world, you may prefer keeping a special locked folder on your computer, or even having a blog, which I also use as a more public form of journal.

One of my good friends keeps her journal on LiveJournal, which does has a private entry option so that only she has the password.

You may be like her and find that you can keep up with your thoughts better when you type. If you're at all like me, I can type faster than I write by hand, and so can my friend, so that is her preferred method of journaling.

I do keep a personal blog of my travels that my clients here, but personally for this exercise, I prefer the good old fashioned cloth book because that way if I am waiting in an airport or out in the middle of nowhere, I can pull it out and jot something down.

If you've never kept a journal before, think of it as a single space where you can write notes or answers to questions in this book and you will be able to keep them all together in a single space. It is very convenient. It is also good to keep the journal with you during the day or even at night, assuming it's the portable kind, so whenever you have a thought or idea about this book or some new inspiring thought, you can jot it down and keep it for later.

The journal you'll be doing for these exercises is a bit too personal for a public Blog, in my opinion, but again, it's all up to you how and what you do – just do it! I promise you will reap the rewards of making this a habit. You never know when that million dollar idea is going to pop in!

Sometimes you will take the notes in the journal, but for the commitment, do it here. Take out a pen and take the first steps toward your ideal you.

I worked for many years representing a famous sales trainer and motivational speaker and one thing they taught us is to work harder on ourselves than we did on our job and everything would always turn out for us.

That is what I am asking you to do here. Realize you are the most important part of this equation. No matter where you've been and what you've been through in your life, today is a new day and it is never too late to begin committing to the things you want out of life.

Statement of Commitment to Live Abundantly & Authentically

I, _____, hereby agree that I will complete this book and the exercises in it to gain a deeper understanding of myself. I will do what it takes to create the abundant life I truly want to live. I understand that this is a process and that it takes 30 days to make a change and I am willing and able to make this commitment to improve my life.

Signed_____ Date_____
Sign your name here

Good job! I congratulate you on taking the first steps toward the new you!

Feel free to take a look back at this every day, if need be, or at any time you feel a little discouraged during the process. I promise you will reap big rewards from doing so!

Seven

To Know Too Much

It seems everyone is obsessed with knowing the future and knowing exactly how things will unfold in life. Certainly in my profession, it seems I'm surrounded by psychics and mystics nearly everywhere I go and there are always plenty of eager patrons who just can't wait for someone to tell them what is going to happen in their future. Who will they marry, what about their love life and how about that big job promotion?

The gift of the Naadi Leaf reading for me was coming face to face with the reality that our desire to know the future is only an illusion because in reality, I discovered that we don't really want to know what is going to happen to us at all.

This topic has been a major pet peeve of mine for years and a consistent theme in many of my books – don't give away your power! You have all the answers within you! And most importantly – I do not believe we can ever fully know the answers to everything, nor would we want to.

When I go out to a lecture, I think people are sometimes shocked that I always say I have no proof of anything I am talking about. Certainly I understand people want to perceive me as some kind of expert, and *I am* an expert on studying the various schools of thought out there, but the reality is that all the books, documentaries and scientific evidence we uncover is all created by us, and since I believe we are living in an unbelievably unlimited universe, I cannot help but to imagine that some of our ideas are quite limited in scope compared to what the creator actually had in mind.

That moment that Naadi Leaf messenger gave my dad's name so specifically, I knew he was talking about me, and there was a sickening feeling that washed over me that is difficult to explain.

"How could they know?" I thought, wondering if indeed we could know the mind of that which created us.

It was like they had me. They knew me. The hand of God himself was now reaching through the heavens and saying, "Hey, you. You think you can hide from me? Well no more. I'm going to tell you everything you ever wanted to know right now."

Had I known they knew so much, would I have asked for this? Of course on some level I believe I did. I think we all choose either consciously or subconsciously what we are experiencing.

The problem was that my friends and I did not initially know just how much information they were going to hand over, and based on the accuracy, it seemed as if they could tell us everything, and I do mean *everything*.

Think about it – would you want to know everything that was going to happen to you? Really give that some thought. Most people I talk to about this answer with an emphatic, "No way!"

During that initial reading, there was an intense and most immediate feeling that these people had information direct from the horse's mouth, so to speak, and that they would tell me exactly what was right, wrong and indifferent about my life as I was leading it.

Those days that passed before we had our full reading created such an intense stir of anxiety within each of us – it was extremely stressful and troubling.

We think we want to know everything, but we don't really find that comforting, it makes us anxious.

The point here is this: you are reading this book to find answers, gain clarity and hope, direction and greater peace in your life, and I pray this will help you in all those areas, but I also want you to remember that life is a journey, not a destination, and that the magic of it is often in the surprising ways things unfold for each of us and it is hidden in the gift of the unknown.

She Cried When She Finally Got Her Goal

Have you ever watched any of the major television award shows like the Academy Awards, Emmys or Grammys? I have always loved these shows, not because I especially enjoy watching a bunch of star-studded celebrities, but because I enjoy seeing people who have struggled to achieve a dream finally make it.

For some reason I will always remember the acceptance speech a few years ago of the Best Actress winner, Halle Berry. Aside from the fact that she was the first ever African- American to win the coveted award, there was more to it than that. She cried and said something to the effect of how hard she worked to get there and how she could not believe it was actually happening, finally, after so much effort.

It is extremely interesting to me to study successful people. You should too, since I know you are interested in success.

A client came in to see me and she was in tears. I wondered what was wrong and was a bit surprised by what she told me.

"I just got my first house," she bawled.

"That's great!" I said, wondering why this would be so upsetting.

"You don't understand," she said. "This is something I wanted for so long – for years."

"Yes, I know…that's great!"

"It's not that!" she continued crying. "It's just that now that it's here, what am I going to do? I mean, I don't have anything else to work for. It's like it's ended or something."

It was interesting to see that the culmination of something that at one point seemed so out of reach is almost enough to make you want to cry when you get it. Is it the hard work and effort that causes this feeling, or is it simply a strange fear that there isn't anything else to go for, or a combination of both?

It reminds me of the Jack Nicholson movie where he looks at Helen Hunt and finally sums it all up, "Is this as good as it gets?"

Life is the journey, and unfortunately, we often don't stop to appreciate that part of it until it is all over. So enjoy yourself and when you arrive on your stage someplace, somewhere in time, you can cry too for all that it took to get there, but be happy! There are always plenty more goals to work toward once that one is finished!

Eight

The Three Things

I teach a class called *Creating the Life You Want* where students are required to make a commitment to attend all the classes and take a deep look at themselves in order to let go of whatever is holding them back so they may move into the life they really wish to have.

This course begins with a lengthy personal questionnaire, included at the end of this chapter, designed to get you thinking in ways you haven't before about your life.

One thing I have been saying for years is that I think that if we want to get really over simplistic about life, there are only three things any of us wants out of our life:

1) Love – What is life without someone to love and without being secure in loving ourselves?

2) Health – I know from personal experience that when you don't have your health, you can't get out of bed to acquire anything else. It is key!

3) Security – In a prosperity class I teach, this thing I call security takes on many forms. For some, it is cash money, abundance and prosperity. For others, it means I have a roof over my head today and plenty of food to eat. From there, money, prosperity, and everything in between are added bonuses. How we feel secure in the world around us is of critical importance to our well-being.

No matter where I go or who I work with, the things they come to talk with me about either in session, in a seminar setting, or in the letters I receive are invariably about one of these three areas, with no exceptions.

By reading this book, you and I have agreed to go on a journey together to help you understand yourself better. There is no better way to do that than by taking stock of where you are, where you've been and where you want to go.

This next part involves you sitting down to a powerful questionnaire designed to help you in all areas of life. I hope you will take the time to do it and to really think about your responses.

It's hard sometimes to admit certain things to ourselves – that we aren't where we want to be, we haven't followed through with things or we just don't like what we're doing at all.

I had to take a hard look at myself, and still do from time to time, because I think that is the only way to make change. You have to know where you are, then accept and come to terms with it, in order to create the space to get where you really want to go.

When I made my life change and quit that job I hated, I had to come face to face with some difficult truths about myself. I was unhappy and unconscious of that fact I did not like what I was doing or where I was going.

You must be at least a few steps ahead of where I was at that time, because you are holding this book. There must be something within you seeking a change, wanting to have a more meaningful and purposeful life. Congratulations! I think awareness is the first step to change and so many are like I was, unaware, going through the motions. So, good job!

She Completely Reinvented Herself and Her Salon

One of my clients was a very successful hair salon owner in Colorado. She had lots of clients and seemed pretty happy, yet within her soul, the seeds of discontent we all feel from time to time began to grow, and grow quickly.

She decided she was tired and wanted out of business. "It is too hard to run my own business," she said. "I just couldn't do it any more."

She had been behind on her rent one month and was just about forced to close the shop when she suddenly decided to close her business and go work for another salon owner, thinking it would be easier to let someone else take the responsibility and deal with the day-to-day operations. She felt it would be better to just show up to work, deal with her clients and call it a day. "With the amount of hours I was putting in, I thought I would end up ahead," she said.

It wasn't even two weeks into her new situation when she realized she had made a horrible mistake and the woman she was now working for had very different values and ways of doing business than she did. "I ran my salon for 14 years," she said. "I didn't realize how hard it would be to have to take orders from someone else."

She came to me at the pinnacle of her crisis and needed help. She wanted out of the mess she created and needed an outside perspective.

"Did the landlord already rent your space to someone else?" I asked.

"No," she said, "I technically still have it until the end of the month, which is another week and a half."

Apparently she had just thrown up her hands and left the place with little prior planning, but in this case, it was to her advantage.

"So you moved everything out?" I asked as she nodded yes.

"Great!" I said, enthusiastically as she stared at me like I had lost my marbles. "That means you can just move back in and call it a Grand Opening!"

"What are you talking about?" she said.

"You told me you rented the place very suddenly, right?"

She nodded.

"So why not deliberately move back in and just call it a Grand Opening – get a fresh coat of paint on the place, rearrange everything and have a party with wine and cheese and if anyone asks, just tell them you decided to remodel and that's why you closed the doors for a couple weeks."

To make a long story short, she followed the advice, and rearranged her space in a way that was new and empowering to her so it felt more like a brand new salon.

As a result, she had renewed enthusiasm for what she was doing since it was like coming to work in a new space. It all turned out for the best.

The point of that little story is this – sometimes we have no idea what we really want, even if we already have it.

Throughout the book you will see more stories of people just like you struggling to get clear and figure it all out, so take light in the fact that you are here now, thinking of these things and working on ways to recreate your life!

Next, I am going to begin the process of helping you figure out what it is that you really, really want to have in your life through a very thorough set of thought-provoking questions I have used with my students through the years to help gauge what you want to work on in your life. Sure enough, as my surveys came in the three areas chosen to work on were:

1) Money
2) Love Life
3) Health

These are listed in the order of most popular responses. This book will address each of these areas as you work from the inside out to decide how to bring more energy and focus into whatever area of your life you presently need work on.

Take out some paper or your journal and answer the following questions as completely and honestly as you can. Remember, you are the only one who is going to see this!

Exercise

1) I define "abundance" as:
2) I define "success" as:
3) I define "gratitude" as:
4) What are your strengths?
5) What are your weaknesses?
6) What about your character are you most proud of?
7) What about your character are you least proud of?
8) What is your greatest accomplishment to date?
9) What has held you back either now or in the past?
10) What area do you need to improve in to feel successful?
11) How do you define success? (internal feelings as well as external factors)
12) What level of success do you want? Describe it then rate it on a scale of 1-10 (lowest to highest)
13) Currently rate on a scale of 1-10 how successful you are.
14) What could you do NOW to make that number higher?
15) What makes you happy?
16) What makes you unhappy?
17) What are you willing to give up to get what you want?
18) What are you willing to change to get what you want?
19) What do you think is the key to success in any endeavor?
20) What area of your life must change NOW for you to live your dreams?
21) Area you most want to focus on – choose one: career, love life, making money, health

That's it, at least for now.

How did you do?

I'm sure if you're like my other students you probably surprised yourself with some of your answers.

Don't be too hard on yourself. That is what this process is for – helping you see yourself more clearly so you can get what you really want from life.

In the next section, we'll start digging deeper as we take a look at what you want and how to get it.

PART TWO
Deciding What You Want

Nine

Passion

After I graduated from college, I decided to enroll in broadcasting school, and to this day, I can say it was one of the best decisions I ever made in my life.

During my time there, I was recruited to work on television programs for ESPN, including several PGA Golf Tournaments and several televised NASCAR auto races.

I enjoyed sports to a certain degree prior to that, but I must say, I became a huge racing fan after seeing the shows from the inside out.

During that time, I met a lifelong friend who profoundly influenced the way I viewed the world and work.

Scott was a freelance sports photographer and his true love was auto racing. The story he told about how he got into his profession was really quite remarkable:

"I had a job I really hated working in St. Louis for a big shipping company. It was just a regular job, nothing special. I always loved the races and I never missed any of them when they came to town." He continued:

"I decided to buy myself a camera and I would go out to the track and shoot video just for myself. It was a hobby I thoroughly enjoyed.

"One day, some cameramen from ESPN came up to me and said, 'Hey! What ya got there? Let us see it.' They looked at my film and said, 'Hey, that's really good! Do you want a job?' and the rest is history."

Scott is an excellent example of someone who is fully following his passion in life. For the past 20 years I've known him, he has traveled all over the United States filming races. He enjoys traveling too, so that is an added bonus to his job.

Was he just 'lucky,' or was this fate or destiny? Certainly I think it was a mix of all three. I think there is something to be said for being in the right place at the right time, but even within that context, he could have told the cameramen that he did not want them to see what he was filming. He could've said 'No,' to the opportunity to work for them as a freelancer.

There is a special mix of opportunity presented to you and your willingness to actually act upon it and do something about it.

Giving Up Something to Get What You Want

While I do not believe that life is a struggle or that you have to make horribly debilitating sacrifices, I do believe that to get what you want, you have to let go of something you have.

In the case of Greg, if he had not been willing to let go of a steady pay check and health benefits to go after his dream job, he would not have been able to create the life he enjoys so much.

Even in love relationships, being with the one you love involves compromise. When two people make a commitment, each has ideas about what they want to do as individuals. When they join, those individual ideas must be meshed together for the benefit of both, right?

Michael is another client of mine who I worked with occasionally over the course of about five or six years. He occasionally needed sessions to talk about his problems and to gain insight into what he described as his horrible marriage to a woman who was cheating on him since before their actual wedding. Her infidelity had continued through the years, and about six months after they were legally married, he discovered that she lied to him about her financial status and had accumulated so much debt that he was now partially responsible for that they would have to declare bankruptcy.

I repeatedly talked to him about his own self-worth, about getting out of this situation so he might find greater peace and happiness in his life.

He was still having these occasional counseling sessions five years into his relationship when I again told him that in order to be happy, it seemed to me like he should finally cut his losses and move on in hopes for a better future with someone who could love and respect him the way he deserved.

His response was, "I could divorce her, but I don't want to lose my cars and trucks. I've worked so hard to get them, I'm afraid if I divorce her I will lose everything."

It was at this point I knew our time had come to an end because I cannot offer any help to people who are not willing to help themselves. Clearly, this man valued his material possessions more than himself and his own well-being, and was not willing to give up something in order to get something more.

We will take a deeper look into this when we get into the section on values, but for now, we can just say that he was unwilling to do what it took to create a life he would really enjoy.

It's not that "sacrifice" should be viewed as a bad thing; it's just an exchange of energy. I believe that if you want something, you have to exchange energy to get it.

We'll talk more about that in the upcoming chapter on profits, but for now, get your journal out and think about the following:

1) What is it that you really feel passionate about?
2) What area of your life would you be willing to change in order to make room for more of what you care deeply about?
3) What things are you doing now that are preventing you from moving forward into your passion?
4) What distractions are you having now?

5) How can you minimize distractions and things you do not enjoy in order to bring more enjoyment into your life?

Next, we'll take a look at a key to understanding how to get more of what you want by discovering why you are here – your purpose.

Ten

Purpose

Earlier in the book you took a brief look at a question I think we all ask ourselves at one time or another – who am I? Why am I here?

These questions are so fundamental to our internal happiness, it is absolutely essential that you take some time now to look into that.

When I work with people to discover soul purpose, I think one of the biggest surprises they have upon discovering it is that it is much simpler than they ever could have imagined.

To think that their purpose is 'to love' or to 'forgive' seems so simple that it often seems almost disappointing to people, but the thing is that life is not supposed to be complicated. The people who master their lives have learned how to do the simple things extraordinarily well, and you are no exception.

She Always Knew

One of my friends is clearly living her purpose and always has been.

She is an incredible artist and photographer whose credits include some of the best known fashion magazines and *People* Magazine.

She owned a photography studio in Malibu, has worked with all sorts of famous people and now concentrates her time and energy on her incredible paintings.

She has been doing all of this since she was only fifteen years old. Some would consider her lucky to have found her passion at such a young age, but as she explained, it wasn't always easy.

"It's been hard at times, but I can't imagine doing anything else," she said. "I always knew it was what I was here for."

It is a mistake to think that when you find that one thing you love most to do that life will cease to be challenging. It always will be filled with ups and downs. I think the key to it all is to do what you love to do most of the time and do your best to be happy most of the time. If you want to know the secret of life, I think that's it!

So let's get busy uncovering what it is that will make you feel most purposeful in your life.

In this next section, you will travel into a relaxed space via guided imagery, where you can easily see and feel what it is you are on this planet for at this time.

Once you understand this at a deeper level, you will have created the space by which you can begin to build your ideal life.

So get ready for this next exercise by finding a nice place to relax for about 30 minutes.

I want to suggest that for this exercise and all other guided journeys in this book that you record yourself reading the instructions, do the exercise with a trusted friend or family member, or memorize the exercise before attempting it. Otherwise, you're going to find it hard to get into the state you wish to attain, because you're going to have to keep opening your eyes to see what you're supposed to do next.

The best way to handle this is to record yourself because your unconscious mind enjoys the sound of your own voice and that is a very personal and powerful way to do these type exercises.

Exercise

So go ahead and sit down and close your eyes and we will begin.

Gently resting your eyes, I want you to imagine there is a beam of pure white light coming down in through the top of your head.

Feel the light moving down, down, down, through your forehead, into your eyes, your nose, your mouth, your jaw and down into your neck.

Feel the light moving into your shoulders, into your arms, your elbows, your wrists, hands and fingertips. Feel it relaxing you and carrying away any tension you have as it begins to move down your spine, through your shoulder blades and into your heart.

Feel the light moving down, down, down, into your stomach, your lungs, breathing in relaxation as it moves down to the base of your spine and into your legs – your thighs, knees, ankles and all the way down into the soles of your feet.

Very good.

Imagine this light is like a waterfall, carrying away all the tension from today and sending it down, down, down and out the soles of your feet and down into the earth.

Imagine the light is getting stronger and stronger and it begins to pour out your heart, creating a beautiful golden ball of light that surrounds you by about three feet in all directions. Very good.

Imagine yourself just floating inside this golden ball of light, safe, secure and totally carefree, feeling very relaxed.

Imagine a beautiful angel is floating down in front of you.

You can either see the angel, feel the presence of this angel or just know the angel is there. Imagine the angel is like a guide to you who knows every single thing there is to know about you, your soul purpose and your mission on earth at this time.

Imagine your angel will take you by the hand now and the two of you will begin now to float. Feel yourself lifting up, up, up, into the air, floating higher and higher and higher into the sky.

Imagine you are just floating away, into the clouds, leaving the world behind as you lift up, up, up...

Very good.

Now imagine you have floated so high in the sky that you are able to look down and see something that looks like a beam of light below you.

That beam of light represents your entire life so far, and all that it will be in the future.

It is as if you have transcended time and space and you find yourself floating above your own life where you can now gain a higher perspective on it.

Imagine that this angel knows every single thing there is to know about you, your soul and your soul's journey and that you have come here today to this space that transcends all time to discover something very important.

As you notice the angel imagine the angel is holding a big ball of light.

In just a moment, the angel will hand you that ball of light.

You have come here today to ask the angel a very important question, and that question is this: What is my soul's purpose?

What is it that I have come here to learn over many, many lifetimes?

Imagine that as you ask it, the angel is handing you that big ball of light and that within that light is all of the energy needed to know the answer to the question right now.

On the count of three you will totally receive this ball of light: one, reaching out, two, the angel is handing this light to you and three, you put that light right inside your heart.

Feel the light as it moves into your heart, your stomach, all the way down your spine and into your legs and feel it move up into your mind so it is now easy for you to know the answer to the question you have – 'What is my soul's purpose?'
　　Imagine you have the answer right now.
　　Very good.

Now that you know why you are here, imagine noticing all the ways you have been learning about your purpose over the course of your lifetime. Allow pictures, thoughts, feelings and memories to flood your mind now as you notice how powerful your purpose is working in your life.

Next, imagine you can think of ways your purpose might work in your future.
In what areas do you think you will express your purpose in the months and years to come? Very good!

Now imagine you can bring all of this information with you as you take the angel by the hand and the two of you begin to come back, through the clouds, you are traveling quickly now; closer to that light which represents your life and the present day.

Feel yourself floating quickly now through the clouds as you feel the gravitational forces of earth bringing you back, down to where you started.

Very good.

You are still surrounded by golden light, safe and secure.

When I count to five you will come back into the room feeling awake, refreshed and better than you did before.

Five, grounded, centered and balanced. Four, continuing to process this information in your dreams so by tomorrow morning you will be fully integrated into this new way of being. Three, driving safely and being safe in all activities. Two, recalling your purpose and noticing daily how you are living your purpose through all your actions. One, grounded, centered and balanced, and you are back!

Good job! So how was that?

Now what I would like you to do is take out your journal and spend a couple minutes answering the following questions.

This will help you solidify what you just experienced.

1) What is your purpose?
2) Were you surprised?
3) How has your purpose been demonstrated in the past?
4) Based on what you know now about what you might like to do in the future, how could you imagine your purpose playing out in the years to come?
5) What do you think is your highest potential?

In the next chapter, we will look at how to profit from what you love to do.

Eleven

Profits

I got a call from a friend of mine the other day who needed to talk. I've known him for about seven years, and ever since we first met, he told me he hates his job and wishes he could do something else.

He purchased a huge half a million dollar home in the ritzy part of town a few years after that initial conversation.

For a bachelor, I had to question his decision. "What are you going to do with such a big place all by yourself?" I asked. "It looks like you're trying to keep up with the Joneses."

His answer was something I have never forgotten. "No, I'm not trying to keep up with the Joneses, I'm trying to surpass them."

He chose to climb the corporate ladder and work the long hours to own all the luxuries and toys he could afford – the Harley, the golf trips to Hawaii with his buddies, the cars, the clothes. In the material world, he had everything, and yet it was obvious to me years ago and still is – something is sorely missing from his life, but what exactly that is, he cannot tell you, even after many years of internal turmoil.

Here we are seven years later and the conversation sounds just about the same, only now, his boss decided to tell him the company is going through changes and they may be laying people off soon.

"I just needed to talk to someone about it," he said. "I may just be paranoid, but I think I might need to send some resumes around. I know several people at other companies who said if I ever wanted to come work for them, they'd love to have me."

"But you don't like what you do now," I said. "Why would you go into that if you don't have to?"

Here is the problem, at least in his mind. This guy has worked for this company for nearly a decade and has built his entire career over the past twenty five years in this industry. He hates it, but he feels trapped and doesn't think there's a way out.

"I don't want to give up my lifestyle," he said, "but I have to admit there are days I wish I could sell everything and move into my mom's house."

Like millions of other Americans who are living right up to the edge of their salaries, this guy is trapped by his own success. He has built such a snare he cannot give up the job he hates because he would also have to give up other things and he is not willing to do that. It all has to do with the way he has aligned his values, which is the subject of an upcoming chapter. Is it right or wrong? There is no judgment; it's just a matter of choice.

I can empathize with where he's at to a certain degree, because it reminds me of what happened to me so many years ago after my friend's death.

To wake up one day and realize you hate your job and need to quit is really an important revelation in someone's life – especially when you realize that you will have to give up a hefty paycheck in order to do it. Yet in his case, for whatever reasons, he is currently unwilling to make the change.

The Grass is Greener

When people come for coaching, most of them are convinced they need to find something they love to do and get paid to do it.

That is all well and good and as we have discussed, it takes effort and willingness to let go of something you have in order to get something you want. Letting go of the job security, stability and hourly pay check to grab the brass ring and create what you really want is an empowering feeling, at least I have found that to be the case.

What sometimes happens though, is that when you go to work

doing something you love, when you take what was once a hobby and turn it into a revenue generating activity, it can sometimes take the joy right out of it.

One client who came in said she was working as a massage therapist and had a huge client list. She felt lost because she was starting to hate her work.

"I got into this because I believe so much in massage and what it can do for people," she said, "only now, I find myself getting tired of it and it seems that I never get to have any massages myself, I am too busy giving them."

The joy was gone, at least temporarily. You've heard stories like this before in many professions – the home builder who creates luxury homes but lives in a horribly neglected home, the hairdresser who lets herself go but makes everyone else look great.

There is no way to be truly successful if this happens to you. I believe you must first give to yourself, love yourself and care for yourself before you can ever fully give to another.

In the case of the massage therapist, I asked her if it would be possible to set aside a few days for herself – no clients, no phone calls or worrying about bills – to go to a spa and splurge on treatments for herself.

"Which place would you want to go to if you could?" I asked her.

She took no time in answering, "Oh, I've always wanted to go to Ten Thousand Waves in Santa Fe," she said. "It's supposed to be the best!"

We got her calendar out and she scheduled a weekend a month later that she drew lines though and she went to the Ten Thousand Waves Spa. When she returned, I asked her to let me know what happened.

"I was like a dream," she said. "I loved every minute of it. It was better than I expected."

"Has it helped you with your dilemma?" I asked.

"It has completely renewed my faith in what I do," she said. "I know I am helping people and I feel better about my work."

So just remember that when you get to the point of this blissful work you enjoy, that in order to continue to enjoy it, you might need to have a change of scenery and an attitude adjustment along the way in order to keep it fresh.

When you think about it, that is the key to success for many celebrities, particularly musical acts. When they have a hit, they must be willing to go on tour and play that same song over and over again for possibly decades to come, and the ones who are most successful are those who keep it fresh so when you hear it and see the performance, they look as though it is just as fun for them and new to them as it was the first time they played it.

Whether it means you take a break from time to time, or pamper yourself, the key to longevity in the area you are most passionate about is often a reflection of your attitude about it, otherwise, just keep it as a hobby and allow that to bring you joy.

She Played the Flute and Recorded A CD

One client was a retired nurse who had recently been widowed when we met. She cared for her ailing husband for many years and was looking to bring more joy into her life. The next time I talked to her was a year later and she said she had taken up playing the flute as a hobby.

She said she had never actually played any instruments before, but now, she felt she wanted to try something completely different from what she had known in her previous years as a wife and mother.

What was amazing is that she was so good at playing the flute, she was invited to play at church and then at the symphony in the little town where she lived. She went on to record a music CD and actually made money doing it.

The beautiful thing about her story is this – she had absolutely no expectation of making a dime from her joy and still it happened anyway. It began as a hobby and turned out to be an incredible, previously untapped talent that she had for music. Through her joy and lack of expectations about where it was going to go, she became wildly successful and joyous as a result.

She is a wonderful example of the fact that the joy in living is not about the money, it comes from doing what we enjoy first.

In the case of money, it is not usually the actual cash you value, but what it means to you. In order to get a better handle on that, please do the following exercise.

Exercise

Please fill in the blanks with the first thing that comes to your mind. Don't analyze it. You are working to get your true feelings out here and since nobody will see this but you, it is important you be honest with yourself.

Money is _____.
Money is _____.
Money is _____.
Money is _____.
Money is _____.

Did you find any of your answers to be surprising? Much of the time, money means security to many people, as I mentioned in the earlier chapter about the three things everyone wants.

Security needs could stem out of being poor when you were young, feeling insecure about where food or other life necessities are going to come from. When you understand why you desire money at a deeper level, you can begin to let go of the fear and create the life you want.

Money as Energy

In my profession, I am around many in the spiritual community who believe money is the root of all evil. That simply is not true. The reason so many struggle to make ends meet is often a deep rooted feeling that it is not okay to have money, but instead that it is more pious to be poor.

Again that is a limiting belief that needs to be cleared. Money is simply energy, nothing more. That's why there is an old saying that money will only make you more of who you already are.

These days, 'prosperity consciousness' is talked about all over the place, but what I mean here is often things that are not conscious, but part of our subconscious beliefs about the energy of money. Sometimes we are actually completely unaware of some of the deep rooted beliefs we have concerning this life enhancing tool.

The Wealthy Worry Needlessly

I talked to a friend recently who was telling me about one of her wealthiest clients who is constantly worried about money. Apparently, to see this woman, she is so extremely rich, many of us would laugh to think she is worried about something she has so much of. If money is making you more of what you are, in this case a worrier can become a super worrier.

I think this generation is very lucky in that most of us have always had a roof over our heads and food to eat. Many of our parents and grandparents were alive during the Great Depression and really know what it is like to not have a thing. That kind of early trauma makes a mark on people that would obviously cause them to worry about things like money, so don't get me wrong, that is okay.

You may have also seen your own family struggle to make ends meet. It is not an easy thing to go through.

The idea here is to get to the bottom of why this is important to you and what it would mean for you to have it so you can begin a healthy relationship with money that will allow you to prosper.

Exercise

1) What does the idea of money mean to you?
2) Does it mean security, freedom, stability?
3) How has your desire for what you think money will bring you helped you or hindered you from having all you want?

Twelve

The Child Within

The challenge of finding our purpose often lies in finding out exactly what that special thing is that we're supposed to do. We've been programmed since childhood to forget our silly ideas and get to the business of growing up and becoming useful members of society.

What we often fail to honor is the wisdom of the child within each of us.

When you were a child, what kind of games did you play? What were your favorite toys?

After working with so many people and helping them get in touch with their highest purpose, I have found it to be incredibly helpful if we can get back in touch with the younger you who remembers and understands why you are here and what your unique gifts, talents and joys really are.

I remember the very first time I took a group through this process. It was a real eye opener for me.

This is a guided journey to meet with the younger you to see what you want to be when you grow up. When I first took a group through it I recall looking out into the pained faces of so many in the crowd afterwards and feeling as though I had gone too far and had done something terribly wrong.

What I came to understand about life is that so many times we feel we have let our dreams die, unfulfilled.

It is often painful to go back and see these things and then have to take stock of how our lives have turned out versus what we envisioned for ourselves as children.

I think one of the major problems comes from the society we live in. We are taught that we have to be the very best or nothing at all. We have to be rich, famous, beautiful, powerful and have all the bells and whistles to go along with that.

What we fail to acknowledge is the journey, as I've mentioned before, and we spend so much of our time focusing on the end result, we lose a lot of joy along the way.

If, for example, you told me you want to be an actor when you grow up, I think there is so much pressure on people that if they can't walk out the door and instantly be as successful as Tom Hanks, then forget it, there is no use in trying.

If it's Not The New York Times, Then Forget It!

I remember I was speaking to a group of aspiring writers one day when this exact subject came up. One lady raised her hand and I thought she had a question.

"I haven't started my book yet," she said.

"Why not?" I asked.

"If I can't be on the *New York Times* Bestseller's list, then I don't want to do it," she said in all seriousness.

This epitomizes exactly what I am talking about here. You have to be willing and able to go on the journey. *Life is not a destination.* If you cannot find the joy in the doing of it, then there is no point and that activity is obviously not for you.

Why can't the aspiring actor find his bliss in simply trying out for a small part in the school play, or tearing tickets at the door or in building sets or handling the lighting or stage direction?

The joy should initially be found in the doing and participating in it, in any way possible regardless of how small or insignificant the role may seem initially.

That's exactly what the flute playing woman from the last chapter did. She had no expectations and did it for the joy of it and for her it worked out, but the point is that if it hadn't, it would have been okay because that was not her reason for playing.

If you are an aspiring bestselling author, you must first find joy in writing and the activities of putting thoughts to paper.

As for myself, I began writing small articles for high school yearbooks, wrote stories for my college newspaper, and eventually became its editor-in-chief.

I had a hard time writing at first because I really had nothing to say, I thought, although I knew I wanted to be a writer someday, I could hardly fulfill the word count requirement for my weekly editorials. Over time and practice I became more proficient in it.

I always knew I would write a book someday, but again, felt I had very little to say. Eventually it happened, thanks to the encouragement from a teacher, and now, the journey continues.

She Built An Empire from a Christmas Ornament

Another remarkable woman I know moved to central Mexico many years ago with her husband because they absolutely fell in love with the area. At the time, she was an extremely successful, and burned out, businesswoman, in much need of the break.

While south of the border, she soon became restless with all of the free time she had on her hands and decided to hand make some Christmas ornaments using only her bare hands, some potters clay and paint.

Since she didn't speak any Spanish and her neighbors did not know any English, she presented the gifts to them and they all just nodded their approval and smiled, thanking her. From that moment on, she was accepted into the community with open arms through her small gesture of friendship.

After the holidays, she was walking around the little town where she lived when she noticed something strange. Everyone was wearing the most unusual necklaces made with the Christmas ornaments she had given everyone.

When she questioned them about their necklaces, an idea was born, and before long, these were being made and distributed all over the country. She has since branched into clothing and has a multi-million dollar business, all thanks to a little holiday cheer.

What you love to do and how you express it in the world can take on a million different forms. It is the joy of doing it, whatever it is, and the one-of-a-kind way you do it that is of value to the world. There is only one you out there and only you can do what you do in a way that brings your special gift out into the world. You really are one in a billion!

So as you go through this next process of meeting with and getting information from the younger you, please don't be sad or disappointed by judging your lack of progress to this point. That is why you are here to discover these things about yourself.

I believe that all things happen when they are supposed to. It's time for you to start seeing that about yourself. You had to go through certain things and have experiences so you could get here now and appreciate where you have been and all that is left for you to do.

Without the less-than-positive things we go through, we cannot appreciate the good things as much and without our prior knowledge we cannot offer the richness of our understanding to those around us.

Please take out your journal and thoughtfully answer the following questions.

Exercise

1) When you were a child, what games did you like to play?
2) If you pretended to be things, what were they? For example, doctor, lawyer, etc.

3) How have you explored your early interests in your career?
4) How have you not fulfilled those early dreams?
5) What did you tell yourself or what happened to defer you from your dream?
6) What do you believe about your ability to do this?
7) What do you do for a living now and how did you get into that?
8) If you could be anything you want to be and salary was not a consideration, what would you do?
9) About work – do you want to be indoors or out?
10) Dealing with the public or working in groups or by yourself?
11) Travel or staying in town?
12) Traditional 9-5 or flex hours?
13) Self employed or at a company?
14) Small or large company?
15) Creative or analytical work?
16) If your childhood dreams can be realized outside of work, what are some ways you could pursue that?
17) Could you take on a new hobby, join a club or participate in different social circles?

Now that you have consciously thought about your childhood, it's time to take a more in depth look at things.

This next exercise is going to require you to use your imagination and go on a powerful journey.

To do this, you will need to find a comfortable place to sit and relax where you will not be disturbed and where you can rest your eyes.

If you'd like, as I recommended before, you can record this process on a tape and play it back to yourself, have a trusted friend read it to you, or memorize it to the best of your ability.

Your unconscious mind loves the sound of your voice, which is why I always recommend you tape it if you can.

Exercise

So go ahead and sit down and close your eyes and we will begin.

Gently resting your eyes, I want you to imagine there is a beam of pure white light coming down in through the top of your head.

Feel the light moving down, down, down, through your forehead, into your eyes, your nose, your mouth, your jaw and down into your neck.

Feel the light moving into your shoulders, into your arms, your elbows, your wrists, hands and fingertips.

Feel it relaxing you and carrying away any tension you have as it begins to move down your spine, through your shoulder blades and into your heart.

Feel the light moving down, down, down, into your stomach, your lungs, breathing in relaxation as it moves down to the base of your spine and into your legs – your thighs, knees, ankles and all the way down into the soles of your feet.

Very good.

Imagine this light is like a waterfall, carrying away all the tension from today and sending it down, down, down and out the soles of your feet and down into the earth.

Imagine the light is getting stronger and stronger and it begins to pour out your heart, creating a beautiful golden ball of light that surrounds you by about three feet in all directions.

Very good.

Imagine yourself just floating inside this golden ball of light, safe, secure and totally carefree, feeling very relaxed.

Now I want you to imagine there is a doorway in front of you. See the door, feel it, or just know it's there and imagine you can open it now and find yourself inside a beautiful room.

Look around the room, notice what's there, feel the relaxing energy in this space and just relax. You now notice there is a doorway on the other side of the room and that doorway is opening now and in comes the younger you – you, when you were a child.

Imagine you can say hello to this younger you and take the younger you by the hand and the two of you walk or float over to the other side of the room where there is a table there and on that table are toys the younger you likes to play with.

What kind of toys do you notice? Take a moment to notice what's there. Very good.

Now imagine you can ask the younger you to show you which toys are the favorites. How does younger you play with these toys? What is younger you pretending?

Ask younger you a question now – what do you want to be when you grow up?
   Imagine you can notice the first answer that comes into your mind.

Imagine you can now recall all the ways in your life that you have expressed these desires and wishes.
   How has your adult life reflected these things you played with as a child?

Imagine you can notice any ideas or thoughts that pop into your mind. Very good.

Now imagine you can thank the younger you for playing with you today and watch as younger you puts away the toys says goodbye and walks back into the door where they came from. Very good.

Now imagine you can take all this information with you as you turn and walk through the door you came in.

You are still surrounded by golden light, safe, secure and totally carefree; noticing that within that golden light only that which is of highest good can come through.

In a moment when I count to five you will come back into the room feeling awake, refreshed and better than you did before.

Five, grounded, centered and balanced. Four, continuing to process this information in your dreams tonight where you will gain even more clarity and insight. Three, driving safely and being safe in all activities. Two, grounded centered and balanced. One, and you're back!

How was that? Interesting, wasn't it?

Now I'd like you to spend a moment reflecting on what you just experienced there.

1) Were you surprised to see the toys you used to play with as a child?
2) Do you see ways you are still using your creativity in your current life?
3) Think carefully about that. You may not be working in that area, but can you see through a hobby or other interest how those thoughts and ideas are being used now?
4) What did you want to be when you grew up? How has that

manifested itself in your life?

5) Again, it may not be your profession, but there may be other ways it is showing up – as a charity, as a hobby, perhaps you have friends in that field. Use your creativity here and I think you will find it has shown up, maybe not as you'd initially envisioned, but it is there.

6) How could you bring more of that passion into your life right now? Could you join a club? Could you bring that into your work somehow?

Because there are so many ways your dreams can express themselves in the material world, it is a good idea to spend some time thinking about what you do on a daily basis.

One Helps Animals and the Other Grows Plants

My students brought me many powerful examples of what I am talking about here.

One woman went on that journey and told me she wanted to be a veterinarian when she grew up. Although she is not a vet now, she does volunteer with the Humane Society, so in a sense, she is living her passion through her volunteer work.

Another woman wanted to be a gardener and ended up working as an architect in her profession designing buildings rather than landscapes. She found great joy by going back to school and taking horticulture classes and is about to graduate with a second degree. She has used her new schooling to create a fabulous garden in her home. Will she eventually turn her profession to landscape architecture? Only time will tell, but when she talks about it, she says she has already found joy in what she has done so far:

"I just love creating these gardens," she said, "I find it my escape, my quiet paradise I have created outside of work where I can really express myself. I just love it."

Clearly, she has found the joy in the journey. That is what it is all about.

He Became a World-Class Knifemaker

My dad is another great example of this. He told me when he was a kid he wanted to be a police detective but his father encouraged him to go into a field he not only found boring, but actually hated, as a chemical engineer so he could take over the family business one day.

He disappointed my grandfather greatly when he left the company and went to work for a manufacturer of Native American crafts and jewelry.

There in that position, now nearly forty years ago, he befriended Native Americans who taught him how to make jewelry and beautiful handcrafted wood items. He became quite an artist and would make everyone wonderful gifts through the years.

He stayed in manufacturing and ran some of the largest firms in the United States through his career and just a few years ago retired and began making amazing custom knives. Now his efforts are hailed as totally unique works of art, and his pieces are coveted by celebrities such as Willie Nelson, Chuck Norris, Tommy Lee Jones, and Toby Keith, as well as many professional athletes.

He told me once how much fun it is to make things for people and wondered why he didn't recognize this sooner.

Again, I believe everything happens in time when it is supposed to, and the appreciation for what he now does is only accentuated by those years in corporate America.

So whatever your bliss and heart's desires truly are, it is never too late to make your dreams reality.

We will continue on our journey to help you develop a plan and a path to get you from where you are now to where you want to go. It is all possible!

Thirteen

Values

Now that we've discussed your passion and purpose and talked to the younger you, we have to touch on what I believe is the foundation to your successful discovery of your life's work — your values.

This area is probably the most neglected and misunderstood aspect of most people; by that, I mean most people don't have any idea what they really value in life, and most are totally unaware that they are unaware. So take heart, dear friend; you are leaps and bounds ahead of the pack, at this point. Congratulations on taking the necessary steps to consciously make a shift!

Your values are at the root of every single thing you do, every decision you make and how you live all aspects of your life. There is no better gift you can give yourself right now that will help you turn your life around more than getting in touch with your core values.

When clients tell me they are unhappy and I begin to ask what they would like to do rather than what they are doing now, most of the time they can't give me an answer. Why? Because the state of mind you are in when you don't know what you want is just another simple way of saying, "I don't know what my values are."

It would seem simple to get to the core of what matters most to you, but the trouble we all have from time to time is discovering what is really within us and what has been forced on us by other people.

We are all influenced by our parents and our upbringing. As we mature, we become influenced by our peers, social groups, clubs or religious organizations, and finally, by our employers.

Is it any wonder with all these inputs going on that we don't have a clue to where we begin and everyone else ends?

When you go to church, you participate in activities that are important to the faith you belong to. When you get a job, your daily activities are based on the values of your company which you are required to follow if you want to work there. When you are in a relationship, you often make compromises in order to be with the other person.

Days weeks and months go by, and pretty soon, you just fall into the daily grind and routine, hardly noticing or even remembering what you really wanted to do way back when. Sound familiar?

This book can certainly help you uncover your passion — what you like to do and what you would want to do if you could — but you will never be able to make forward progress in that unless you have a clear idea about your core values and ensure those values are in alignment with what you are passionate about.

She Doesn't Want a Husband

One very successful client came to see me recently. She works as a consultant, travels all over the world, has friends everywhere and runs a successful company, yet something was missing.

"My parents have been getting on me lately about getting married," she said. "They told me if I don't change my life, I will never find anyone."

This discussion with her parents had apparently been playing repeatedly in her mind and had been bothering her.

"Is there something wrong with me?" she asked.

"No, of course not," I said.

"I do want to meet someone, but I still have a lot of the world to see," she said.

This is a perfect example of how other influences around us cause us to question or even change our values in order to meet the status quo or fit in.

We took an assessment of her core values and when we did, it was obvious that she was indeed living authentically according to the values she said were most important to her including: freedom, adventure, recognition and success.

What she was able to see about herself is that if she continues to value these things most as her core values, then a committed relationship would be difficult if not impossible to attract because it was not even on her list!

If you've been reading the latest theories you know that what you think about expands. That is a fundamental law of the universe.

In this case, this woman was a beautiful example of living a free and adventurous life.

If relationship should become important to her in the future, she would need to realign at least one core value in order to attract that to herself.

I am not advocating changing her entire personality; I am talking about altering a core value. It would be important for this woman to continue to value adventure and success, while adding commitment and love to the list, if and when it something she truly wants to create. By not compromising her own core values, that way, the partner she attracts will be someone of like mind and the relationship could flourish.

It is also important to realize you do not ever need to apologize to yourself or anyone else about what is important to you.

She Doesn't Want a Career

Another woman came to see me recently specifically to work on her values. "I think I'm messed up somehow," she said. "I just can't seem to get motivated and I want to make changes in my life."

I asked her about her job which she said she'd had for about six months. She told me it was quite enjoyable. She had worked herself out of a sales position she really didn't like and now she was a technology trainer.

Her explanation did not sit well with me. I sensed some kind of discontent there, although I was not sure where it came from.

After putting her through some of the exercises you are about to go through, it was easy to see that she valued relationship and friendship and love but things like power, achievement and success were not even on her list at all.

I pointed this out to her and she told me about a new relationship she was in but expressed concerns that it would not work out, fearing it would be ultimately disappointing like so many others from her past.

What was uncovered is that she really does not care about advancing at work and was putting undue pressure on herself to climb the corporate ladder.

What she really wanted was to find the right partner and a committed relationship so she had spent the last several months joining groups of like-minded people in order to meet new friends who would share similar interests. It was there that she met this new man in her life and there were discussions of the relationship becoming more serious.

"You don't have to want to run the company," I said. "You are just fine the way you are. You have a great job, you do it well, and if I were you I would be at peace with that and concentrate on what matters to you – your friends and relationship."

Instantly her posture straightened up, her jaw relaxed, and I could tell she needed to hear she was okay, just the way she is.

I'm here to tell you that you are also okay just the way you are. You are allowed in this wonderful country we live in to be and think and do whatever you want to and you have nobody to answer to about that but yourself.

He Found Solace in His Friends

Another man who had a few sessions with me came in to tell me how sick he was of his job and the long hours he had to work during the holidays.

"You sound like a broken record," I said. "You are in a retail business, you know that from November through the end of the year you have to work overtime, so you can either quit your job and go elsewhere, or you need to accept the fact that this is the way it is here and learn to deal with it."

What came out of this session was no different than any other – this man valued the friends he made at the company more than the work itself. I pointed out to him that if he left the job, he would most likely lose touch with his friends because they would no longer have that bond of a common workplace.

We had to get in touch with his values so that he could get things into a new perspective. Most of the year, he enjoyed the job, for the most part, and he had reasonable hours. He valued his friends most of all — much more than the work — so he needed to realize that in order to keep what he valued most, he needed to make a few sacrifices, like doing some overtime in the holiday months, in order to gain what he wanted most: his friends.

We discussed this earlier in the chapter about passion: sometimes you have to be willing to give in order to get. In this case, the man calmed down, changed his perspective of anger, and realized he was thankful to have so many wonderful friends at work. It was worth a couple of Saturdays of overtime to keep what he cherished so much.

It all comes down to what you value. Then you have to weigh it out, make your own choice about what is most important to you and put your energy and attention into that.

The thing is, you have to become *aware* of what is most important to you so you can then begin to make adjustments in attitude and activity to create what you want in life.

What makes you happy is uniquely you and that is amazing!

Remember that as we go into this next section. I'd like you to do the following values assessment.

It is important in this part to allow your first impressions to be your answers. Please don't judge yourself or change an answer just because it sounds better to do so. You are fine just the way you are!

In this exercise you will be able to have a clearer picture of who you really are so you can move forward toward living the life you deserve.

Exercise

The following is a personal values assessment. Please rate each item on a scale of 1-5, 1= very important 2= important 3=somewhat important 4=not important 5= definitely not important. Remember to allow the first thing that comes to your mind to be your answer. It is best not to 'think' too much about this for better accuracy. Let's begin.

Remember, very important is number 1, not at all is lower down the scale.

Achievement	1	2	3	4	5
Advancement	1	2	3	4	5
Adventure	1	2	3	4	5
Appearance	1	2	3	4	5

Arts	1	2	3	4	5
Authority	1	2	3	4	5
Challenge	1	2	3	4	5
Charity	1	2	3	4	5
Competition	1	2	3	4	5
Communication	1	2	3	4	5
Community	1	2	3	4	5
Country	1	2	3	4	5
Courage	1	2	3	4	5
Creativity	1	2	3	4	5
Democracy	1	2	3	4	5
Diplomacy	1	2	3	4	5
Efficiency	1	2	3	4	5
Environment	1	2	3	4	5
Ethical practice	1	2	3	4	5
Fairness	1	2	3	4	5
Fame	1	2	3	4	5
Family	1	2	3	4	5
Friendship	1	2	3	4	5
Fun	1	2	3	4	5
Harmony	1	2	3	4	5
Honesty	1	2	3	4	5
Integrity	1	2	3	4	5
Intelligence	1	2	3	4	5
Intimacy	1	2	3	4	5
Knowledge	1	2	3	4	5
Loyalty	1	2	3	4	5
Money	1	2	3	4	5
Nature	1	2	3	4	5
Peace	1	2	3	4	5
Personal Growth	1	2	3	4	5
Power	1	2	3	4	5
Recognition	1	2	3	4	5
Religion	1	2	3	4	5

Security	1	2	3	4	5
Self-Respect	1	2	3	4	5
Serenity	1	2	3	4	5
Spirituality	1	2	3	4	5
Stability	1	2	3	4	5
Status	1	2	3	4	5
Teamwork	1	2	3	4	5
Tolerance	1	2	3	4	5
Tradition	1	2	3	4	5
Wealth	1	2	3	4	5
Wisdom	1	2	3	4	5
Work	1	2	3	4	5

Now before you go back and change your answers, if you did this correctly, some of your gut responses may be surprising to you. Please don't judge yourself and know that you are free to think, feel and be whoever you want.

You may notice that some of your values are quite different than they were a few years ago. That's fine too. Values shift and change as we change, which is another reason why this exercise is so valuable to do every year or two.

One troubling thing I see is when clients want to apologize for the answers they put down on the values assessment. There is no need to be sorry for the way you authentically feel about something!

If you don't find charity at the top of your list right now, that's fine! No need to beat yourself up over it. You will get to it if you are meant to do that. If it is truly something you want to do, then at some point in your life you will consciously make that value a priority. Honor where you are because that is the first step in beginning to create the life you want to live – no apologies necessary.

To further your progress on this subject, do the next exercise, which shows a list of two contradictory values. Your job will be to circle the one that seems most like you – again, without thinking too much about your answers. Just do the first thing that comes to mind, ready?

Exercise

Please circle the choice that most closely reflects your desire or value.

1) Love or Money?
2) Democrat or Republican?
3) Conservative or Liberal?
4) Black, White or Gray?
5) Capitalism or Socialism?
6) Charity or Greed?
7) Fame or Quiet Solitude?
8) Spontaneity or Predictability?
9) Independence or Union?
10) Stability or Change?

Next, we need to go deeper with our understanding of the first two exercises so I would like you to take out your journal and take some time answering the following questions:

Exercise

Go back to the values assessment above and write a list of every value you marked with the number 1. These represent your core values.

If you have more than five core values, please eliminate some until you get to your top five.

Now rank the top five in order from 1 to 5, one being that which is most important to you and then rewrite your list so it is in the proper order. Again, don't think about it, just do it so you are honest with yourself without judgment.

Now go back to the assessment and write down anything in the list you marked with the number 5. Just take a look at this list and notice that these are things you said are absolutely not important to you at this time when, you hopefully made the list from your first impressions.

As you notice the concepts in the 5 group, are you surprised by what you see? Is there anything there you thought you valued, yet you don't?

Can you see a pattern or contrast between the types of things you value and the types of things you don't?

If you love and highly value family, community and intimacy and you don't value achievement, work and status, yet you find yourself spending all your time at the office, can you see how that would be a value conflict?

On the other hand, if you value adventure and personal growth yet you are stuck at a boring desk job, can you also see how that could be a conflict?

Take time to look and see if there are any glaring conflicts between what you truly value and how you are currently living your life. Please take time to think about this and write down your impressions.

Last, make sure the values you selected are yours, meaning they are not those of your parents, your peers, your boss, or anyone else. You have a right to think and feel what you want so make sure these values are a reflection of that.

Remember there are no right or wrong answers here. By being honest with yourself, you are likely to uncover a source of your unhappiness or conflict so you can move into a space of greater inner peace.

This book will help you resolve this conflict, if there is one, and I think it is better to know if there are conflicts in your life than to be completely unaware.

Now is a good time for you to carefully consider how your life reflects your values. If family is important to you and you are with someone who does not want a family, can you see a conflict there?

If honesty is important and you have friends who lie to you, can you see how that is a conflict?

Take some time to think about your values and how they are reflected in your life. Get your journal out and write about it and reflect on it for the next few days. I think you'll be surprised by what you'll discover about yourself.

Part Three

How to Get What You Want

Fourteen

Gratitude

Early on in the book, you made the commitment to undergo massive change and grow, and the next step to ensure your success is to express gratitude for all you have.

I would imagine you are not reading this book because every little thing in your life is just perfect. On the contrary, it is normally when life is not going so good that we turn to education, other people and books to help find answers.

Yet what I am saying is so important to consider as often as possible. Even if you hate your job, your relationship is the pits or you want a new place to live, there are still many things you can be thankful for right now.

Before you can ever get more in life you have to take care of what you have and one of the best ways to do that is through the practice of gratitude.

I received a gift once called the Five Year Journal from a friend of mine. There was a note in it from the author of the journal talking about 'How to Make a Gratitude Journal.' The steps were simple enough – every night before bed or before you start your day, simply write down you are most grateful for.

If we turn our attention to the concepts of quantum physics which teach that what we focus on expands, then to focus each day on what we are grateful for only causes there to be more things we can begin to notice to find thanks in.

Some days are tough, I am not going to say they aren't, and some days it is harder than others to feel grateful. It is a discipline and that discipline eventually becomes a habit.

On those not so great days, I often write something like this:

Today I am grateful to have a roof over my head.

Not too inspired, yet it is true that when things aren't the best, you realize you still have it better than many people in other parts of the world! Count your blessings!

Don't get me wrong, most days, I am thankful for friends, family and the life I enjoy; it's just that not every single day is a bed of roses. I'm sure you can relate.

Ironically, several months after I first started this practice, the flyer I first read fell from my Gratitude Journal and I realized that this 'gratitude journal' was merely a suggestion on how to use the book and not necessarily what the book was for. It did not matter to me, though, because I am still using this every day and it has made amazing changes in my life and my outlook, and I know it will help you.

If at some point during our time together you have a tough day, and I'm sure it will happen at least once during our time together, then so be it. Honor it and be thankful for the smallest things.

I think life is like the rolling tide in the ocean called existence. Sometimes you are so high up there you feel on top of the world and you know there is nothing going to bring you down. Then, out of the blue, you find yourself in the pit of despair and wonder what happened. Seemingly not of your own actions or volition, there you are, sobbing your heart out.

I have found that by understanding the cyclical nature of life, the ebb and flow of things, you can learn to accept things as they are and the highs, while high, will not lead to the crash and burn of hitting rock bottom.

I like to think of it as finding a way to go from a raging stormy sea to calm waters and a gentle breeze. You still have ups and downs, yet the crash downward is something you accept and because there is peace within, you find things are much easier to get through.

She Learned to Get Out of a Slump

I have a dear friend who told me she used to suffer from deep depression. "I used to stay in bed for days," she said, "I couldn't function sometimes."

"How did you get out of it?" I asked.

"I just learned to let go and allow myself to feel down once in awhile," she said. "I think I was prolonging the agony and beating myself up over the way I felt and that was causing me to feel bad much longer than when I learned to accept it. Now if I have a bad day, I allow myself to go take a nap, no guilt, no worry, and normally when I get up, I feel much better and then I feel thankful."

It is amazing how feelings of gratitude can transform even our darkest hours.

In this next exercise, I want you to get in touch with your own feelings of appreciation.

The first step for you is to sit down with your journal and write about things you feel grateful for. Spend some time with this one and really write in detail not only about what you are thankful for, but why.

Exercise

What are you most grateful for right now and why?

In the area of your job or livelihood, what are you most thankful for and why?

In the area of your health, what are you most thankful for and why?

In the area of family, friends or loved ones, what are you most grateful for and why?

What are you most grateful for regarding where you live? Your country, your home, and why?

Very good! I hope you took some time with these to deeply express thanks for what you have now so that it may expand and multiply.

Next, I would like to challenge you to keep your own gratitude journal during the time we spend together. Pick a time of day, either before you start the day, noon time or when the day is done and spend just a minute or two writing down what you are grateful for that day.

Try a little exercise with me now to see how easy this is. Ready? Get a pen and paper and answer the following:

1) Today, I am grateful for _____.
2) Today, I am grateful for _____.
3) Today, I am grateful for _____.
4) Today, I am grateful for _____.
5) Today, I am most grateful for _____.

See how easy this is? All I am suggesting is writing one thing per day. It only takes moments, yet it sets the course for the big picture of your life and allows you to receive more than you ever knew was possible. Do it today! I know what you will find is that your reasons for joy and thanks will expand as you begin to notice these things more consciously.

For me, I find that keeping my gratitude journal right next to my bed at night prompts me to jot a few words right before I go to sleep. That way it gives me just a moment to look back at the day and find something to find joy in.

The power of doing this exercise before you go to bed is this –

your mind will work on the things you look at last while you sleep and so you have many hours to subconsciously process your thanks and I can tell you from experience, what you think about will expand and your blessings will be greater than ever before!

So keep your journal and enjoy the journey of blessings!

Fifteen

Breakdown to Breakthrough

While we are on the subject of learning to roll with the tides of life, there is a very profound and important concept I would like to talk to you about.

I call it *'breakdown to breakthrough.'*

By 'breakdown,' I am not necessarily talking about a full-blown nervous breakdown trip- to-the-mental-ward kind of medical psychological experience, although I am also not excluding that as a possibility.

The truth is that in our society, unfortunately, we have trained ourselves to be motivated by pain and suffering. You may be reading this and saying it isn't so, but I am sure if you look back over the past decade, if you are being honest with yourself, you will surely find at least one or two incidents where you waited too long, ignored a problem or situation until it was literally screaming at you and you had to take action. Let's face it – we've all been there.

If life is a bed of roses, we tend to become complacent and rest on our laurels. In many cases we won't act until there is some form of pain being threatened either to our security, or our pocketbook.

When all is well, we don't pick up the self-help book, we don't go to the class, attend the lecture or talk to the counselor. We usually do those things only when things are less than perfect. It's just human nature.

I am convinced more and more that our over-stimulation from TV, video games, the internet and all of our technological advances, not to mention the constant bombardment the media exposes us to every minute of our lives is completely overloading our brain capacity.

Your brain is like a computer and just like your computer needs time to process, your brain also needs some downtime to reboot and organize all the programs running in it 24 hours a day, seven days a week.

The problem is that none of us are ever given the proper amount of downtime. We are completely overloaded in every possible way.

When I spoke in the last section briefly about our lives being like the ebb and flow of the tide, I mentioned that often we are in stormy seas with all heck breaking loose around us and everything completely out of control.

To get to a space where the sea of life is calm like a warm spring afternoon takes some discipline and often some changes in lifestyle.

To discipline yourself to do the things you don't want to do before your life gets out of control is something that helps that sea stay calm.

The other thing I have found to be quite profound is silence. Yes, you heard me – silence. It really is golden, just like they say, only it is one commodity that is so difficult to find these days.

I plan to take groups on silent retreats in the future to give people a taste of what I am talking about.

A mild example of the power of silence happened to me just over the summer.

I went to Colorado for a trade show and afterward I was guided to go rent a cabin in the woods all alone, cell phone switched off and no computer for four days.

The first afternoon when I arrived, I was in heaven. The cabin was cozy and wonderful and I was happy to 'get away from it all.'

That night, I built a fire from scratch – a task I hadn't done in years, and I enjoyed a simple meal I cooked for myself.

I stared into the fire and watched the embers crack until the last log was burned to a stump, then I went to bed.

By this time, just to give you a clear picture, I was only about eight or maybe nine hours into my silence. All was going great until I woke up suddenly in the middle of the night.

The thoughts that raced through my mind were disturbing, to say the least. I found myself thinking all kinds of things like, "I have to get out of here," and "I should go stay with friends, this place is horrible."

The loud banter in my mind created a frenzy of fear and panic and I sat up in my bed literally in a sweat.

I got up and got a drink and began to consciously listen to what I was thinking. Then something interesting happened. I became truly aware of the fact that the things in my mind were not real. They were illusions my mind created because it was obviously tired of being alone and wanted someone to talk to.

I decided to break my own silence by talking aloud to myself: "It's okay, everything is fine." After repeating this, I began to calm down and was finally able to get to sleep and stayed that way until morning.

At that moment, I realized something important had occurred. I had undergone a little mental breakdown. My mind, the computer, had finally run through all the data and in the last ditch effort for control, my ego or conscious mind, was racing through the ugly depths of some unconscious programming, or negative self-talk, if you will.

Once I stayed with it, totally in the moment and allowed myself time to work through it and began reprogramming what I was thinking, I was once again at peace. The second day my thoughts slowed down until I was aware of each thought as I thought it.

As the days went on, I found myself feeling joy and true presence in the simplest tasks.

I find myself from time to time feeling a tiny panic over various situations and I now recognize it for what it is – sensory overload. When I feel like that, I know I must go into silence and meditate until the feeling is gone. By doing that I am not ignoring it, I am allowing it — actually being okay with the thoughts and allowing them to come and go and then replacing them with other more positive thinking.

This single process has given me more peace than just about anything. I know you also could use the gift of silence from time to time.

The trouble is, how are you going to take that time? It can be a simple as spending an afternoon in the park, with cell phones, pagers and Blackberry's off limits.As I discovered, it does not have to be for a long time.

During my stay at the cabin, my little "breakdown" occurred just eight hours into my journey.

I know we are overloaded and I think this would be a tremendous gift you can give yourself. I would request that at least one time during our eight weeks you carve out eight to ten hours of time when you go off and be alone and still and allow your mind to run its course. It is a powerful process.

On a similar note, I think the benefits of meditation are also useful in this regard. I am a big proponent of Transcendental Meditation, a process I have talked about in my other writings that I truly feel changed my life.

When I was first initiated into the process, I recall my mind was like a spinning top, I could feel my nervous system unraveling as I slowed down to the process. It was incredibly powerful.

I highly recommend everyone practice some kind of meditation, even if it's just five minutes of closing your eyes at the beginning and end of the day. It does wonders.

As powerful as meditation is, I still think silence for longer periods of time and being alone with yourself and your thoughts is something entirely different altogether. I cannot tell you how much this is of benefit to me at least once every three months.

Exercise

1) Sit in a quiet place and close your eyes.
2) Imagine feeling relaxation wash over you
3) Begin breathing in through your nose and out through your mouth
4) As you continue to relax, allow thoughts to pass through your mind.
5) Imagine the thoughts you are having can slow down and become less frequent
6) After your mind unwinds a bit, imagine that the only thing you can think about is your breathing – in through your nose and out through your mouth.
7) Next allow yourself to relax even more as you simply enjoy the feeling of being relaxed
8) Stay in this space for at least five more minutes, breathing and allowing yourself to fully relax
9) Continue to practice this and go for longer periods of time. Notice the more relaxed you feel, the more you can notice new thoughts coming in that may be filled with new ideas and inspiration
10) Write down any inspiring thoughts so you can take action on them later

Exercise

Sometime during the next month, I would like to challenge you to go into silence somewhere out in a natural setting for at least four hours.

If you are concerned you live in a city and there is no place to go, think of a zoo or an urban park. Just someplace where you leave your cell phone, laptop, Blackberry and all forms of communication to the outside world behind and you allow yourself to think and be.

Preferably, if you can get out of town to do this like I did, that would be wonderful, but if not, just do the best you can. When I am on business trips, even in New York City where there are millions of people all around me, I can still find some form of silence because I am normally by myself and have my own thoughts to myself. You could go to Central Park and walk through the trees, or whatever.

Just be in a setting where you are alone with your own thoughts for some lengthy period of time. You will truly be amazed at how powerful this is!

Sixteen

Removing the Obstacle of Fear

Speaking of breakdowns, the next section will help you to break down what I know to be the biggest obstacle to your success – *fear*.

There is no telling how many multi-million dollar earth-changing ideas there are out there just floating in someone's head or sitting in a desk drawer somewhere gathering dust.

Why we are afraid to take action on certain things is beyond me, yet I know it to be a very complex and multi-dimensional state of mind.

There are sometimes deep subconscious reasons why we fail to do all we can do, to live up to our potential or to grab the brass ring.

I think that for the most part, there are only three things that we are afraid of including:

1) Our own success – What happens to you if you become too successful and your friends don't want you any more? You have to work too hard? You don't get any time off from work? You may not be able to juggle the demands on your time with home, family and work?

2) Failure and humiliation – What is failure, anyway? I personally do not believe it even exists because how can you fail if you do something and it is not correct? Don't you learn from it so you can do it better the next time? And who in their right mind would judge you for trying something? There is no harm in it and you just might succeed!

3) Injury or death – Certainly there are legitimate things we must be at least a bit fearful of in order to stay alive, such as burning your hand on the stove, car accidents, falls from high places and so on. Fear can be used for self-preservation but what tends to happen is that things that would not actually kill us have sometimes been miscategorized in our minds to be life-threatening, when indeed, they are not. I think that comes from the days when we were living in caves. In those days, there just might be a wooly mammoth about to run you down, or a vicious animal barring its fangs and about to choose you for dinner.

These days, those things so rarely happen, it is other types of fear that gets our adrenaline going and scares us out of taking action to get where we want to go. If you ask your boss for a raise and he says no, is that a life or death situation? No, it isn't, and yet internally we are so stressed out about even the prospect of doing it which we run over and over in our minds that by the time we get around to it, we are literally scared to death – for no good reason.

I Now Love Bumpy Flights

Because I chose, to a certain extent, to take stock in what was said during my Naadi Leaf reading, and use it as a basis for creating my reality, having someone else say I will be on earth well into my nineties has given me a profound sense of inner peace.

Is it real, or imagined? I am not to say because I really do not know. All I can say is that I feel it deep within myself that my life will be long and my health will be good most of that time, so I do not sweat the small stuff anymore.

I was talking to someone recently about the fear people get when flying in airplanes these days. I was on a trip and had to stop over in Chicago where the weather is not always the best.

The plane circled for over an hour in a snowstorm before it was able to land, and I remember a time when I would have been scared to death of that. On that day, though, I felt at peace.

I could practically feel the fear of everyone around me, yet I was calm and centered because I knew I would live to tell about it. All was well.

Do I choose to believe it? Yes, I do. I am creating my reality after all, just like you are, and as a big fan of quantum theory, I know we get what we think about.

I now consider the leaves as a tool to help me create – a sort of blueprint I can follow and I must say I have a deeper level of peace than I ever have, and a renewed feeling of knowing I still have many years to explore everything life has to offer and that the soul which is eternal will go on from here.

I would imagine that fear has given you a few stumbling blocks along the way at some time or another and this section is designed to help clear out some of those deep inner anxieties within you.

Before we begin the guided imagery, I would like you to take your journal out to jot down answers to the following:

1) What scares you most?
2) Is there a good reason why that should scare you?
3) If not, what can you do to relieve yourself of this unnecessary fear?
4) How has the fear prevented you from attaining a goal or objective?
5) What can you do now to make a change?

Next, go ahead and get ready for another guided journey. You may want to record it.

Exercise

For this exercise, you need to find a comfortable place to sit where it is quiet and you can relax for a few minutes. Again, if you would like to record this in your own voice and play it back, that would be great! So let's begin.

Sit comfortably and gently close your eyes. Imagine a beam of pure white light coming down through the top of your head.

Feel the light moving into your forehead, your eyes, nose and mouth, feel it moving into your jaw, down, down, down into your neck and shoulders.

Imagine the light is moving down into your arms, your elbows, wrists, hands and fingertips.

Feel the light moving down your spine, into your shoulder blades and down into your heart. Imagine this light is relaxing you and healing you and carrying away all the tension from today as it continues to move down, down, down all the way to the base of your spine and into your legs, your thighs, knees, ankles and all the way down to the soles of your feet.
Imagine the light is like a waterfall just pouring through you carrying away your tension and it begins to get stronger and stronger and it pours out your heart creating a beautiful golden ball of light that surrounds you by about three feet in all directions.

Imagine yourself floating, peacefully inside this golden ball of light, safe, secure and totally carefree knowing that inside this golden ball of light only that which is of your highest good can come though. Very good.

Imagine there is a beautiful angel who is floating down in front of you. You can either see the angel, feel the presence of the angel or just know an angel is there.

Imagine the angel takes you by the hand and the two of you begin now to float, and you feel yourself lifting up, up, up, higher and higher, off of the ground, floating high in the sky, up, up, up, imagining that the higher up you float, the more relaxed you feel.

As you continue to float higher and higher and higher you find that you have floated so high in the sky that as you look below you, you notice something that looks or feels like a beam of laser light and that laser light represents your timeline, or the way that you sort time.

Imagine you are floating over today and you can look out into the future and notice how bright the future is.

Now imagine you can turn and look back toward the past, and imagine as you do, that the past gets lighter and lighter and lighter. Very good.

Now in just a moment you and your angel are going to float back over the past to the source event of any fear you may have that is holding you back from where you want to go.

Remember you are still surrounded by golden light, safe, secure and totally carefree, begin now to float back, further and further back, going to the source of any fears you are ready to clear right now.

And by the time I count to three you will arrive at this source event. One, floating back, back, back, two, further and further, and three, you're there, and you are floating down, down, down, into that event and imagine you can notice what's happening as you remain surrounded by that golden light and completely relaxed.

Notice the source of the fear. Can you see that it's not needed anymore? Very good.

Imagine your angel is sending a beam of pure white light down over those events, healing and relaxing everything until there is only peace. Take just a moment to feel this peaceful light surrounding you, very good.

Imagine that peaceful light has healed that fear and then feel yourself lifting up, up, up, out of that event, floating over your timeline and imagine you can float back toward now, but only as quickly as all events between then and now can totally realign themselves with this new energy.

By the time I count to three, you will once again be floating over today. One, floating toward now, two, further and further, and three, you're there.

Notice how much lighter you feel as you take the angel by the hand and begin to float back down toward the earth, coming back through the clouds until you land, back where we started. Very good.

You are still surrounded by a golden ball of light, safe, secure and totally carefree, knowing that within this golden ball of light only that which is of highest good can come through. Very good.

In a moment when I count to five you will come back into the room feeling awake, refreshed, and better than you did before. Five, grounded centered and balanced. Four, continuing to process this new peaceful energy in your sleep tonight so by tomorrow morning you will be fully integrated into this new way of being. Three, driving safely and being safe in all activities. Two, grounded, centered and balanced, And One, you're back!

Great job! Feel free to use this exercise more than once. The fears we have that hold us back are often many and can be tamed easily through these type of exercises.

Seventeen

Forgiveness

You've heard the old saying about insanity – doing the same things over and over again and expecting a different result. Then in times like these when you are making change, you have to take a look back sometimes in order to move forward and you have to be willing to forgive yourself for making mistakes, repeating bad habits and all of that.

You have to get to a point where you are okay with it and you come to accept that everything happens for a reason and brought you to where you are now and all is well and as it should be.

For that, you need forgiveness.

Of course, you also have to be willing to let go of that horrible thing your mom told you when you were a kid, or that time your dad made a promise he didn't keep. You have to stop making excuses for why you aren't moving forward.

Everyone has hard times. It's what you do with them that counts.

No matter how horrible your past was and whatever went on there that either you did or someone else did to you, right now — today — is the time to let it all go and move forward.

By this point in the book, you have worked really hard on yourself. You have waded through the tons of stuff stored up in your mind and you have hopefully discovered some very powerful things about you and what really matters most.

All of that is wonderful and you are doing a great job, but it won't do you any good if you continue to beat yourself up over the past and forget to let go and forgive.

When you hold on to that old stuff and all those nasty programs from the past, it takes so much of your energy away from you — energy you could be using to create the life you really deserve. The life that is within your reach right now!

I want to share a powerful exercise with you that has not only helped thousands of people I've worked with, but it has helped me too, more than I can ever express here. It is a guided imagery journey you will take to a space where you can release old emotions and forgive others.

You will be amazed how much more energy you have after this one, let me tell you!

Exercise

For this exercise, you need to find a comfortable place to sit where it is quiet and you can relax for a few minutes. Again, if you would like to record this in your own voice and play it back, that would be great! So let's begin.

Sit comfortably and gently close your eyes. Imagine a beam of pure white light coming down through the top of your head. Feel the light moving into your forehead, your eyes, nose and mouth, feel it moving into your jaw, down, down, down into your neck and shoulders.

Imagine the light is moving down into your arms, your elbows, wrists, hands and fingertips.
Feel the light moving down your spine, into your shoulder blades and down into your heart.

Imagine this light is relaxing you and healing you and carrying away all the tension from today as it continues to move down, down, down all the way to the base of your spine and into your legs, your thighs, knees, ankles and all the way down to the soles of your feet.

Imagine the light is like a waterfall just pouring through you carrying away your tension and it begins to get stronger and stronger and it pours out your heart creating a beautiful golden ball of light that surrounds you by about three feet in all directions.

Imagine yourself floating peacefully inside this golden ball of light, safe, secure and totally carefree knowing that inside this golden ball of light only that which is of your highest good can come though. Very good.

Imagine there is a beautiful angel who is floating down in front of you. You can either see the angel, feel the presence of the angel or just know an angel is there.

Now imagine there is a doorway in front of you. You can either see it, feel it or just know it is there. Go ahead and imagine you and your angel are walking through the door and step inside a beautiful room.

Imagine you can look around the room and notice what's there, feel the peaceful energy of this space as you notice what's there.

Imagine there is a doorway on the other side of the room and that door is opening and here come your parents. Imagine they are smiling and happy to see you and that this is their higher self, the very best of who they are.

They have come today to either apologize to you or to receive your apology, or just to tell you how much you are appreciated so take a few minutes and talk to them.

Very good, now imagine you can easily forgive them, and they can easily forgive you and you can now recognize that everyone was just doing the best they could at the time and all is well.

Now imagine there is an energetic cord of light that is coming out your solar plexus or stomach area and it is connecting you to them. This cord represents any disagreements or things from the past that no longer serve you.

Your angel is carrying a big pair of golden scissors and in just a moment, when I count to three, your angel will cut that cord and release all that has happened in the past, knowing that today is a new day and all is well.

Ready? One, two, three, cut! You feel a lightness as you let everything go and a beautiful light is floating into the room and into your stomach and all the way up to your heart, healing you, relieving you and making you lighter than before. Very good.

Imagine mom and dad are getting this same energy and they become so light that they simply float away, back through the doorway from which they came.

Now imagine the door swings open once again and here comes the one person in the entire world who most needs your forgiveness right now.

Notice the person, again as their higher self, or the very best part of who they are, and imagine they are coming to you now and telling you how very sorry they are for what has happened.

Imagine sensing the sincerity in them and take just a moment to hear and understand what they want to say to you.

Now imagine there is an energetic cord of light that is coming out your solar plexus or stomach area and it is connecting you to them. This cord represents any disagreements or things from the past that no longer serve you.

Your angel is carrying a big pair of golden scissors and in just a moment, when I count to three, your angel will cut that cord and release all that has happened in the past, knowing that today is a new day and all is well.

Ready? One, two, three, cut! You feel a lightness as you let everything go and a beautiful light is floating into the room and into your stomach and all the way up to your heart, healing you, relieving you and making you lighter than before. Very good.

Now imagine they can receive this energy also and become lighter than before, thanking you and floating back through the door where they came from, very good!

Next, you notice the most important person of all is coming through that doorway – you. Imagine you can say hello to yourself and I want you to now express your forgiveness to yourself for anything you did not do, did not try or anything else that needs to be discussed. Take a moment to talk to yourself about things that you feel are unresolved and forgive yourself.

Now imagine there is an energetic cord of light that is coming out your solar plexus or stomach area and it is connecting you to yourself. This cord represents any disappointments or let downs from the past that no longer serve you.

Your angel is carrying a big pair of golden scissors and in just a moment, when I count to three, your angel will cut that cord and release all that has happened in the past, knowing that today is a new day and all is well.

Ready? One, two, three, cut! You feel a lightness as you let everything go and a beautiful light is floating into the room and into your stomach and all the way up to your heart, healing you, relieving you and making you lighter than before. Very good.

Imagine you see yourself feeling lighter and offer yourself unconditional love. Feel your heart opening as you extend loving feelings to yourself and tell yourself once again how wonderful you are and that all is as it should be, all is well. Very good!

Now you see a lighter version of you turning and floating away, back through the door which your other self came in from. Very good.

Now turn and go back the way you came and walk through the door, leaving the room behind and find yourself back where we started.

You are still surrounded by a golden ball of light, safe, secure and totally carefree and in a moment when I count to five you will come back into the room feeling awake, refreshed and better than you did before.

Five, grounded, centered and balanced. Four, continuing to process this information in your dreams tonight so by tomorrow morning you are fully integrated into all this new energy you now have. Three, driving safely and being safe in all your activities. Two, wiggling your fingers and toes and starting to come back. One, grounded, centered and balanced, and you are back!

How was that? I have found this to be one of the most powerful processes I ever do with people. When you open your heart to forgive others, you allow the divine to flow freely in your life and bless you in many amazing and sometimes unexpected ways.

Congratulations on completing this process!

You may wonder what good it is to do such things in your mind regarding those who have wronged you in the past. I can tell you both from personal experience and from the experiences of hundreds of clients that this process, although it is in your mind, has incredible implications with your loved ones in your life.

Her Long Lost Brother Gave Her a Call

There are literally too many cases now to count of people who did processes like this with me and had a loved one who they had not spoken to in years literally pick up the phone the day after they did this and call to apologize.

One particular case that stands out is about a woman who had not spoken to her brother since their father's funeral five years before. She came in the office, went through the process you just did and was surprised her brother showed up and they forgave each other. That very next day he called her out of the blue, so to speak, and apologized.

Her Dog Thanked Her

One interesting story was about a woman who also did this process and her little dog who she had just put to sleep had come in to tell her he was fine and to thank her for doing what she needed to do to care for him in that way. He was happy and playing and was so thankful. She came out of the process feeling a deep sense of relief.

As I am sure you are aware, there are many things in this world which are unexplained and to think that our experience is limited only to the five senses and what we see in the physical world is a rather limited perception of all that is in our creation.

Just like our dreams often give us information in symbology or otherwise about things that are to come or how to resolve difficult states of mind, these processes are similar. When you go into an altered state and open up your creative mind, you are tapping into an unlimited wealth of energy and information that is felt and very often accepted energetically by those you love.

So good job! I challenge you to do this exercise more than once if you need to, or just go in your own mind and imagine anyone else you need to resolve things with walking through that doorway. You will be so happy with the results.

I also challenge you to pay attention to your encounters with these people over the next days, weeks and months and see if you can notice any shifts or changes in attitude.

There is an old saying that we need to heal the part of us that is other people. If it is true that we are all connected to each other, and physicists are actually confirming that fact for us now through science, then it is true also that there is a part of you that is everyone else so when you go inside, change the way you see someone or feel about someone, whether they are in your presence or not, you will make a real change in the world.

You may not notice anything right away, but I promise you that one day you will have something happen and you will stop and say, 'Wow! Was that ever a change!'

Be open to it and see what happens. Good luck!

Eighteen

Patience & Perseverance

The only way to succeed is to stick with it – regardless of what it is. If you have a dream, a vision, you owe it to yourself not only to go for it, but to stick with it and see it through.

There is an old saying that you cannot rush the river, you cannot make the grass grow, it happens in its own time.

Like the people you've been reading about in this book, the dream is most definitely possible if you can hang in there while it all lines up and happens.

If you're like me, you wanted it, and you wanted it yesterday. It is okay to be anxious, to a certain degree, but again, it is about the road you're on and the journey, and sometimes that journey cannot be rushed.

She Cleans Houses & Writes Books

One of my most remarkable friends is also one of the most underestimated people I know, at least in the eyes of her peers.

By day, she works cleaning houses of the wealthy, but by night, she is an incredible writer who has an amazing gift with words.

She understands something I tell my students – if you have to work for others in a job that is not what you want to be doing, do it joyfully and realize that they may own your time, some of the time, but they do not own your mind. That is yours and yours alone.

While she is dusting a piece of furniture or waxing a floors, her inner world is quiet and it is there that she is able to create the wonderful ideas for her books.

"One of these days I'll be able to leave this kind of work

behind," she said, "but in the meantime, I just try to enjoy it as best I can and know something better is coming."

No matter where you find yourself in life, once you are on your path, hang in there and allow the things you want to create to become illuminated in your life.

The Mailman is a Millionaire

You cannot judge a book by its cover. I know you have heard this one before, and yet there is another man I know who is a rich and successful investor who works as a mailman during the day.

What his customers do not know about him is that while he is slipping your water bill into your mailbox, his blackberry is in his pocket and he is making millions in the stock market. Buy, sell, trade, put letters in the box. It's that simple, and he is doing it every single day. He enjoys driving around, visiting people in the local community, and he also likes his employee benefits, even though he really doesn't need them any more.

Who says you cannot work a 'real job' and still enjoy your passion while making a profit? It is all possible!

Nineteen

Keep Your Own Counsel

I am convinced the only reason why people suffer is because of the way they view reality. If you can somehow go inside and change negative thoughts to positive ones, your life can turn around overnight – no exceptions.

One of the most detrimental things I see people do, and have done myself, is to listen to other people's opinions. When that happens, you not only suffer from your own view of reality, but from the confusion arising from so many different points of view.

I stopped asking others for advice a long time ago when I finally realized that for every ten people you ask about your problem you get ten different answers.

There is a deep need within us to be accepted and to have people like us. For some people this need is greater than others and I think that is something I have personally had to come to terms with through the years. Luckily my career in sales and marketing early in life gave me a thick skin and the ability to realize that rejection is not all about me.

Still, for many people, we really want others to value us, we want to feel accepted and we also wonder if what we are doing is the correct thing so we ask others what they think.

There was an old saying we learned in my days in sales training that goes like this:

Never take advice from anyone more messed up than you are.

Sounds silly, but I think the advice is sound.

How can any other person know what is right for you when you are, as I said before and I will continue to say, a totally unique one-of-a-kind creation? Nobody but you knows for sure what is right for you. Period.

Recently I got into this again when I was making plans to take a trip. I told a few people about my upcoming voyage and got several unsolicited opinions about what I should do and when and where I should go.

I became so frustrated I didn't even book my ticket until weeks after I first made my decision to go. I was weighing everything that everyone else was saying about what I was doing. It drove me nuts.

Finally, I got wise to what was happening and I shut the phones off for a day and meditated. I asked the only guidance that is ever reliable — my inner self — and booked the ticket that evening.

I was wound up and paralyzed over a simple plane trip. It makes me wonder what happens to each of us on a daily basis when we are dealing with issues much more important than that, such as whom you should marry, what job you should take, and so on.

These huge life choices are yours and yours alone to make and nobody has the right to 'should' on you without your permission.

Only in the quiet of your deepest inner space can you find the answer that truly makes your heart sing.

I find myself doing a lot of this type of damage control with clients who come in to the office telling me that somebody told them this or that and now they do not know what to do. "What do you think?" I ask them, and invariably they tell me they do not know, or they explain why they were not able to take action on something based on what so and so said to them.

It's the same type of thing I was struggling with regarding my travel plans. How many times have you sacrificed a deep cherished desire based on the attitudes and fears of other people? Answer that question, and then please don't beat yourself up over the answer. Remember, we've all been there! This process is about recognizing what happened before and letting it go to create something new.

I want to take you through a little exercise I find quite helpful when discerning whether or not something is right for me.

Exercise

Sit in a comfortable space and begin to breathe deeply, relaxing more and more with every breath.

Now think about something you need to make a decision on in the near future.

Think about all the options available to you and if you need to, write them down on a piece of paper.

Think of the first option. Hold that thought in your mind. How does it feel? Do you feel any tension in your body? What about your heart? Can you feel any energy in your heart?

Repeat this process for any and all options that you have. Once you are finished, go back and do it again, only this time be quick about it and notice only one thing – which option warms your heart?

This is not easy to do at first. We are so out of touch with our feelings in this society it is sometimes difficult to have feelings at all and when we do, we often dismiss them.

I want you to recognize what scientists are now documenting as fact – your heart has an innate intelligence within it and it is the *very best* screening device for your decisions.

Please take your time with this until you can sense, if even barely, the warm feeling you have that is just slightly different from any other option available to you.

When you feel it, know that is your answer and do not question it. Go with it. To follow the heart is the wisest thing of all to do – no exceptions.

Once you make that decision, stick with it and move forward. Know that all is well. Remember to keep your own counsel and allow your heart to make the decisions for you. Get in that quiet space often and your life will begin to unfold more magically than ever before.

Carthusian Coordinates Exercise

Another exercise you can do to help work problems out to your mind's satisfaction, and figure out what to do in any given situation, is called the Carthusian Coordinates, an exercise I learned many years ago that has helped me tremendously. It is supposedly named for a contemplative order of nuns who use it as both a meditation and a problem solving device and it will be helpful for you too.

Here it is:

1) Think of the issue or problem at hand.
2) Hold the image, thought or feeling in your mind.
3) Answer the following questions about it:
    a) What would happen if I did?
    b) What would happen if I didn't?
    c) What wouldn't happen if I did?
    d) What wouldn't happen if I didn't?

Now the answer should come easier because these questions assist you in 'getting out of the box' by stimulating different parts of the brain. Again this exercise can be used to loosen up the mind so you can more readily feel the inner wisdom of your heart.

Try it. It works!

Part Four
Putting it All Together

Twenty

Your Best & Brightest Future

Now you have worked though your fear of success, you've let go of old grudges and you have forgiven yourself, and you have an idea of your core values, your passions and your purpose in life.

This next part is my personal favorite because this is where we put it all together by taking a guided journey into your brightest future.

I have been doing this kind of work now for many years and it is incredibly powerful.

In this process you will actually imagine yourself out in the future creating the life you want to live and actually living the life you deserve!

This will prepare us for the very last stage which will involve your action plan.

I want to leave you with actual concrete steps you can take to get you from where you are now to where you want to go.

When you have a clear vision of what it looks like to be happy, successful and at peace, then you will be more likely to create that, providing you can understand exactly what needs to be done.

One other thing is this – I want you to be as open to this process as you have been throughout our journey together.

When you go out and see or feel yourself in that brightest place, it is so important that you actually believe that what you are seeing, although it is part of your imagination, is actually possible.

There is an old saying, 'if you can see it, you can believe it,' meaning if you can think of something in your mind, then it is possible. Everything is possible!

Sometimes it is hard to see the forest through the trees and we all get discouraged from time to time, but everything really is possible! You can do whatever you set your mind to.

She Visualized Her Retail Store

About a year ago, I had a client who wanted to go through extensive weekly coaching sessions for six weeks in order to help open herself to her intuition and create a new, more empowering future. She had an advanced degree and was working as a college professor, but felt there was something else she was called to do and could not quite figure out what that looked like to her.

She was not at all in touch with her inner guidance when we first began working together, and she did not even know how to even begin to meditate.

I am so proud of her because once I taught her a few simple techniques, she immediately opened up and began having very profound visions.

On the week we did the session about futures like what you are about to do in a moment, she quickly traveled into her brightest future to a place where she could see herself in a retail store.

She described everything about the place, the color of the paint on the wall and the exact time it was going to open. Sure enough, within three months, everything she saw had come to pass – exactly as she had described it.

Now she has a thriving business in our community that is one of the best-known shops of its kind in the whole Dallas-Fort Worth area, and it all started with her own vision.

How was she able to create such a wonderful new life for herself in literally three months flat?

There is only one word for it – *belief.*

The biggest problem I have with people is getting them to believe that the things they see in their mind's eye are indeed real, or at least possible.

So many times people will travel to that place, like you are about to do, where they are happy, healthy and living the life of their dreams, and when they get to that space they talk about how wonderful it is there and then they completely disempowered themselves by saying something like, "Well, it's probably just my imagination," or "I don't know if I could really do that. I must be making it up," or "I'm just seeing this because so and so told me they could see me doing this. It isn't real."

You get what you think about. I know I am beginning to sound like a broken record here, and yet it is true. The biggest gift you can give yourself is to believe that the things that are in that special place in your brain called your imagination are actually true and then follow your own action plan to get there.

Believe me, there is absolutely no scientific evidence to let us know that what we are seeing and experiencing on a daily basis is real or not so why not choose to think your little fantasies in your mind's eye are real? That's what I do!

He Doesn't Take His Own Advice

A friend recently told me something about myself. He said, "Shelley, you know what the difference between you and everyone else is? When you have a fleeting thought run through your mind, you actually do something about it as though it's real. I have that kind of thoughts all the time, but I assume they are only my imagination, so I don't pay any attention to them."

My advice to him was, "Start paying attention!"

And that is the same thing I am telling you now. Why not follow those incredibly wonderful little thoughts in your head to see where they lead you. You might find yourself suddenly and inescapably living the life of your dreams. That wouldn't be so bad!

So let's do this process now – I know you will love it. It is without a doubt the most revealing process you can ever do, particularly after all of the preparation work you have done to get to this space.

As you go through this, I want you to either consciously or subconsciously recall all the new things you've learned about yourself during the course of this book.

Hopefully by now you've rediscovered what you wanted to be when you grow up, you've tapped into things you are passionate about and you have removed any fears or nagging self doubts that were previously hindering your success, and most importantly, you have a new understanding of your core values and the things that matter most to you so you are ready now to take a look at your brightest future, putting all these things in place as you totally recreate your life right before your eyes.

So let's begin.

Again, you need to find a comfortable place to relax where you will not be disturbed for about fifteen minutes. You can record this process if you'd like and play it back, okay? So let's begin.

Exercise

Sit comfortably and gently close your eyes.

Imagine a beam of pure white light coming down through the top of your head. Feel the light moving into your forehead, your eyes, nose and mouth, feel it moving into your jaw, down, down, down into your neck and shoulders.

Imagine the light is moving down into your arms, your elbows, wrists, hands and fingertips. Feel the light moving down your spine, into your shoulder blades and down into your heart.

Imagine this light is relaxing you and healing you and carrying away all the tension from today as it continues to move down, down, down all the way to the base of your spine and into your legs, your thighs, knees, ankles and all the way down to the soles of your feet.

Imagine the light is like a waterfall just pouring through you carrying away your tension and it begins to get stronger and stronger and it pours out your heart creating a beautiful golden ball of light that surrounds you by about three feet in all directions.

Imagine yourself floating, peacefully inside this golden ball of light, safe, secure and totally carefree knowing that inside this golden ball of light only that which is of your highest good can come though. Very good.

Imagine there is a beautiful angel who is floating down in front of you. You can either see the angel, feel the presence of the angel or just know an angel is there.

Take the angel by the hand and imagine the two of you are beginning to float.

Floating up in the air, higher and higher and higher, up, up, up, into the clouds, just floating away, higher and higher, up, up, up, knowing that the higher up you float, the more relaxed you feel. Higher and higher and higher, up, up, up... Very good.

Now imagine you have floated so high in the sky that as you look down you notice something that looks or feels like a beam of laser light. That laser light beam represents your time line, or the way that you sort time.

You are floating over today, this present moment, and I want you to imagine you can turn and look out in the direction of your future and notice how bright the future looks.

And as you notice the future it gets even brighter, and brighter than before, very good.

Now from this space, imagine your angel can remind you of your soul's purpose, your life mission and the reason why you are here at this time.

Spend just a moment thinking about all the ways you have already been living that purpose – lessons you learned, people you met, places you've been, all leading you to this moment. Very good.

Now imagine you can turn your attention again toward your future, noticing how bright that future is. In just a moment you and your angel are going to journey together out, over your future to an unspecified moment in that future where you are happy, healthy and successful and where you are successfully living your purpose.

So let's go there now.

Take your angel by the hand and the two of you are beginning to float, out over that future, further and further out, into the future in your current lifetime to a place where you are happy healthy and living purpose and on the count of three you will arrive at that special moment.

One, moving out, out, out. Two, further and further, almost there. And Three, you're there, and you float down, down, down into that event and imagine you can notice what's happening there.

So what year is it? Allow yourself to notice the first thing that comes to your mind. Where are you? Notice the first thing that comes into your mind. What's happening there? Take a moment to really be there and notice what is happening.

How do you feel? How does it feel to be successful, happy, knowing you are fulfilling your mission here on earth?

Imagine you can remember all the steps you took to arrive at this incredible time in your life. Notice how easy it is to remember how you got here because *you've already done it*.

So what was the first step you took to get here? And then what did you do? And what happened next? Go ahead and notice how easy it is to recall the steps you took to get to this successful space you are now in.

I want you to really tune in now to the feeling of what it feels like to be so happy and successful, to know that everything has worked out even better than you could have ever imagined.

As you get into those feelings, I want you to imagine your subconscious mind can give you a symbol, or a thought or visual image that represents this feeling you are now having. It could be a flower, a butterfly – anything you want, just notice that symbol, again allowing the first thing you think of to bubble up into your mind now.

Very good. Now I want you to imagine that anytime you see this symbol out in the physical world or you think about it in your mind that you will be instantly drawn back into the space where you are right now – recalling your success, feeling happy and knowing you are on purpose.

Now take these feelings with you now as you lift up, up, up, out of that event and floating back toward now, toward today until by the time I count to three you will once again be floating over today....one, two, three, you're there, and you are floating over now.

Now imagine you can take the angel with you as you float down, down, down, back through the clouds, down, down, down, until once again you land, back where you started.

You are still surrounded by a golden ball of light – safe, secure and totally carefree, knowing you can keep this light with you always and that within that light only that which is of your highest good comes through.

You can take all of the energy you need to feel awake, refreshed and better than you did before, but any excess energy will begin to float now, down, down, down through the soles of your feet and down into the earth.

You are grounded, centered and balanced and in a moment when I count to five you will come back, feeling awake, refreshed and better than you did before.

Five, grounded, centered and balanced. Four, continuing to process this information in your dreams tonight so by tomorrow morning you are fully integrated into this new energy and way of being. Three, driving safely and being safe in all activities. Two, grounded centered and balanced. And One, you're back!

Next I want you to write down your experience so it will be easier to recall all of the insights you received in the last exercise so please take a minute and go on to the next chapter. You'll be glad you did!

Twenty One

Action Plan

Now that you had the opportunity to experience your brightest future firsthand, I want you to have the steps to your success clearly solidified – not only in your mind, but in your journal so it is easier to execute your plan.

The next section is designed to assist you in developing a step-by-step roadmap to take you where you want to go. It is probably best to write this out in your journal or wherever you have kept your other notes so it is easy to refer to and you can keep it.

The biggest reason why people do not make change is because they have no idea of where to begin.

In the last section, you received some powerful information from your subconscious mind about your future destiny and I want you to take this time to recall it in writing so it is easy to look back on as you begin this new chapter of your life.

Exercise

1) During the course of our time together, what did you discover your values are?
2) What is your passion or thing you enjoy more than anything else?
3) What is your purpose as you now see it?
4) During the exercise of going into your future, where did you go and what did you see or experience there? If you did not actually have an experience, please take this time to imagine what your brightest future would be if you were allowed to just make it up.
5) Describe your feelings about this special space and what it meant to you to achieve your objective.

6) To the best of your ability, please recall the very first thing you did to make that dream a reality.

7) Imagine you could write an action plan that would start tomorrow. What could you do tomorrow that would help you move toward this special place in the future?

8) What things would you do next week that would further your goal?

9) Next month, what kinds of activities will you do to further your goal?

10) Next think about a year from now and every other year between now and the place you imagined in the future. Can you notice how each step led you to where you wanted to go? What were some of the major objectives you did to create this reality?

11) Is there anything else you need to write down that is important to this process? If so, please write it here.

12) Recall the symbol you saw or created in your mind that represents your successful outcome. Please draw that symbol now, to the best of your ability. Remember that any time you see it, draw it or think it, you will be reminded of your brightest path.

That's it! I hope you will refer back to this action plan as often as you need to get from where you are today to where you want to be. Several months down the road when you look back on it, you will find it interesting to notice just how far you've come in a short period of time. Remember that the path begins today with that very first step.

Twenty Two

Conclusion

I predict over the next decade we are going to see a massive exodus from what we've considered for the past 50-60 years to be the traditional workplace.

More people are going to return to self-employment, hopefully doing things they really enjoy, so now, more than ever, is the time for you to understand what it is you enjoy doing and begin now to make the change before the change is made for you.

Is there some higher destiny or higher power guiding us through our journey called life? I believe there is and that within that framework, you also have the power within to make your journey the best it can be. It's all based on your attitudes, thoughts and feelings about your life and where you want to go.

Now that you understand what you value most in life, know that you are fine just the way you are. There is no need to apologize for who you are, you should rejoice in it and know that you are bringing something very special to the world that only you can share.

As the world we live in continues to evolve and shift, you will find more people around you who feel as you do about the world. More chance to connect with others as we all shift back to a place of knowing and recalling that we do need and appreciate each other.

There is a wonderful story I heard recently about a woman who took a spiritual journey to Egypt and when she got there she just knew she was going to have something very mystical and profound happen to her there.

She ventured into the inner sanctuary of the Great Pyramid at

Giza, and sat there very somberly waiting for her big epiphany to arrive.

Just as she was at the height of her meditative state, something funny happened. A little boy came up to her from out of nowhere, lifted her skirt and laughed playfully as he ran away.

Someone asked the woman, "So, what did you learn from that?"

"The "enlightenment" I received was that I need to lighten up!"

What an incredibly powerful message, applicable to us all.

Take time to enjoy your life and what you are doing here on earth at this time. Make the most of each day and commit to doing it in joy, because when you are joyous, you change the face of the world with your exceptional presence.

Bibliography

Canfield, Jack *The Success Principles: How to Get from Where You Are to Where You Want to Be.* Harper Collins: New York: NY, 2005.

Chopra, Deepak *Creating Affluence: The A to Z Steps to a Richer Life. Amber-Allen Publishing, Novato: CA, 1994.*

Chopra, Deepak *The Seven Spiritual Laws of Success: A Practical Guide to the Fulfillment of Your Dreams. Amber-Allen Publishing, Novato: CA, 1994.*

Clason, George S. *The Richest Man in Babylon.* Penguin Books, New York: NY, 1988.

Covey, Stephen R. *The Seven Habits of Highly Effective People: Audio Seminar.* Covey Leadership Center, Provo: UT, 2004.

Eker, T. Harv. *Secrets of the Millionaire Mind: Mastering the Inner Game of Wealth.* Harper Business, New York: NY: 2005.

Eker, T. Harv. *Speedwealth: How to Make a Million In Your Own Business in 3 Years or Less.* Peak Potentials Publishing, Vancouver: BC Canada, 1996.

Hill, Napoleon *Think and Grow Rich, Aventine Press, 2004.*

Hopkins, Tom *How to Master the Art of Selling,* Warner Books: New York: NY, 2005.

MacKay, Harvey *Swim With the Sharks Without Being Eaten Alive.* Harper Collins, New York: NY: 2005.

McGraw, Phil *Love Smart: Find the One You Want – Fix the One You've Got.* Simon & Schuster: New York: NY, 2005.

McGraw, Phil *Self Matters: Creating Your Life From the Inside Out.* Simon & Schuster, New York: NY, 2001.

Ray, Paul H. and Sherry Ruth Anderson, Ph.D. *The Cultural Creatives: How 50 Million People are Changing the World.* Three Rivres Press, New York: NY: 2000.

Robbins, Tony *Unlimited Power.* Simon & Schuster: New York: NY, 1986.

Rohn, Jim *Take Charge of Your Life, Nightingale-Conant Corporation, Chicago, 1991.*

Trump, Donald *How to Get Rich: Big Deals from the Star of The Apprentice.* Random House: New York: NY, 2004.

About the Author

Shelley Kaehr, Ph.D., has spent her entire career in the field of human potential, first as a top representative for internationally renowned sales guru Tom Hopkins and motivational leader Jim Rohn, and has since become one of the world's leading authorities on the mind-body connection and world renowned hypnotherapist, having worked with dozens of leaders in the field of consciousness and optimal potential.

Shelley has a private coaching and consulting business in Dallas, Texas, and is a sought after speaker in the corporate world.

Visit her online at

www.shelleykaehr.com
or
www.sales101book.com

BOOKS

O is a symbol of the world, of oneness and unity. In different cultures it also means the "eye," symbolizing knowledge and insight. We aim to publish books that are accessible, constructive and that challenge accepted opinion, both that of academia and the "moral majority."

Our books are available in all good English language bookstores worldwide. If you don't see the book on the shelves ask the bookstore to order it for you, quoting the ISBN number and title. Alternatively you can order online (all major online retail sites carry our titles) or contact the distributor in the relevant country, listed on the copyright page.

See our website **www.o-books.net** for a full list of over 500 titles, growing by 100 a year.

And tune in to myspiritradio.com for our book review radio show, hosted by June-Elleni Laine, where you can listen to the authors discussing their books.